THE CALL WIZARD

Everything the novice or professional needs to know
to build and increase success in communicating with others
by phone or in face-to-face meetings.

John Peaker

Eloquent Books
New York, New York

The Call Wizard
Copyright 2007 by John Peaker

Eloquent Books
An imprint of Writers Literary & Publishing Services, Inc.
845 Third Avenue, 6th Floor – 6016
New York, NY 10022
www.eloquentbooks.com

ISBN: 978-1-934925-02-7 / SKU 1-934925-02-0
PCN: 2008922163

Printed in the United States of America

Design: Mark Bredt

Photo/Illustration © Simon Moore / Agency: www.DreamsTime.com

Introduction

How many times have we said, or heard others say, "If I could just get in the door?"

"The Call Wizard" is where it all starts with a complete, highly effective communications strategy.

Through this guide, you will learn everything the novice or professional needs to know to build and increase success in communicating with others by phone or in face-to-face meetings.

It is of crucial importance that you retain a completely open mind through each and every chapter. It is of equal importance that you do not deviate in any manner from the proven techniques. Although you may feel somewhat unfamiliar at first, persist and persevere through that initial pain barrier. The old adage, "no pain, no gain," is particularly true as it relates to the cold call.

Give yourself 90 days to hone your presentation call skills. Practice diligently on a daily basis, and you will be successful in achieving any and all goals.

Whether you are an individual who is considering sales as a career, a person who has been involved in sales for any number of years, any individual seeking employment or a professional who must market their services to others, the contents of this guide will launch your career to new heights.

The methodology in "The Call Wizard" can be easily customized by any individual in any field of endeavour who has to make a cold call, send an e-mail or write a convincing letter for any purpose. As you are selling yourself to someone every day, it is critical that you master the skills of the acting profession with the skills of a professional sales person.

TABLE OF CONTENTS

I.   PROFILE OF A SUCCESSFUL SALESPERSON

Whether your career objective is directly in sales, or - as is the case of many professional consultants - in establishing accounts to service, selling skills are what will determine your ultimate success. Your first prospect communication sets the stage for the degree of success that follow.

Selling is the highest paid profession in the world. If you aspire to become a part of it, then you must first pay your dues. You must be prepared to put your time, your heart and soul, and some of your own money into an investment - yourself. If you truly believe you are your own best investment, then you are ready to walk through the door leading to the most exciting, the most rewarding, and the most vital profession in the world.

You are obviously interested in learning how to sell - or how to sell smarter - or you wouldn't have put out your hard-earned money to purchase this guide. Be assured that such a small investment will pay huge dividends in changing your life for the better, if that's what you're seeking. Its contents, if used wisely, will not only help guide you, but will also enhance your career and sales opportunities.

Let's take a glimpse at some of the necessary traits that you must acquire, develop and refine over a period of time if you are to achieve truly professional status.

To be successful in the selling profession you must, first of all, believe that you're the world's greatest salesperson. You must repeat it over and over again until you believe it. The number one product that you are selling is YOURSELF. Don't ever forget it! You can accomplish any goal if you believe in yourself and want success badly enough. Believing in yourself is only one aspect in becoming successful. You also must have a burning desire to commit yourself to learning the skills of the trade and the product knowledge to speak with authority.

One of the greatest boxers of all time, Muhammad Ali, truly believed that he was the greatest - and he proved it. In many of his fights he looked almost fragile in physical appearance when compared to some of his mammoth opponents. He psyched himself into believing that he was invincible and that he couldn't possibly lose. Ali, had more going for him, however, than just his belief in himself. He was superbly conditioned and learned his trade through countless hours of preparation.

He learned all aspects of his profession through endless practice and study then more practice. Muhammad Ali became the greatest because he learned and practiced all the boxing skills and techniques taught to him by his mentors. He became a well rounded boxer with a strong offence, and an impregnable defence.

One of Ali's strongest attributes was his ability to listen. He listened to his trainer, Angelo Dundee, who planned his every move in the ring. Ali would then execute the fight plan to perfection. He was sold on number one - himself - and reinforced his own belief in himself through acquired skills.

Everyone, regardless of their chosen profession, at one time or another, becomes involved in the selling process.

Selling Is Theatre

Have you ever seen that little kid at the check out counter? Sure you have! He's doing weird gyrations on the floor, screaming at the top of his lungs, arms and legs flailing in all directions. He's a screaming, mean salesman doing a selling job on his embarrassed mother, who wishes she could vaporize. That child is acting out a role to get what he wants.

He knows that he is on center stage and that he is playing the leading role. And so it is with all of us at one time or another. Whether we realize it or not we all become actors when we are trying to sell something.

At this very moment, some eager salesperson that is fired with energy and commitment is making a sales pitch that will result in failure. The presentation will fail because the person lacks the knowledge in selling techniques and has misread the personality of the person to whom he is selling.

The mission of this guide is to teach you how to become the epitome of a well-rounded successful salesperson, with the acting abilities of a professional troubadour. Whatever intelligence, talent, and imagination that you bring to this undertaking must be properly moulded and manipulated to suit your audience - The Prospect.

If you like people, possess drive and intensity of purpose, you will be able to develop skills that will lead you to sales excellence. Just as the theatre is a place where an audience comes to be amused, interested, entertained, stimulated or moved by the enactment of a play on a stage, you also are expected to entertain in order to be successful in the sales profession.

Like the actor you, the salesperson must overcome attitudes and the attention span of the audience. The stature of many actors or salespeople is measured by their ability to surmount any and all obstacles that prevent the achievement of the desired effect.

The performer - actor or salesperson - has three basic elements with which to work: the contents of the play or presentation, the sequence of the play, and the delivery of the contents. To become a complete sales professional you must be adept at delivering all three elements in a dramatic manner that your audience will remember and believe.

Unlike the actor, whose job is completed with the delivery of the script, or presentation, the salesperson's role has just begun. You will encounter objections that must be overcome, and, you will have to close the sale on your own. In subsequent chapters, you will learn effective script techniques, correct presentation skills, how best to overcome objections, and closing skills that really work.

Personal Attributes Required for Success

Stamina

The dictionary defines stamina as strength and endurance, the ability to withstand hardship or difficulty.

Stamina as it relates to the sales profession requires a high energy level, combined with the durability of a long distance runner. Like the runner who hits the wall in a marathon, you must go beyond the pain barrier if you are to achieve your goals.

Unless you have accomplished the feat of running 26 miles, 285 yards, you can't imagine the feeling of utter ecstasy that is experienced upon crossing the finish line. You must be willing to make that one extra call late in the day even when you feel like quitting. Like the runner who hits the wall, you must go beyond the pain barrier if you are to achieve your goals. And like that runner, you will experience a sudden rush of adrenaline and sense of invincibility with that next successful call. You will succeed only if you make that next call. It is a great feeling of accomplishment.

People Oriented

Salespeople that show a genuine interest in customers' needs and work at solving their problems are generally the top sales producers. They know that by going that extra yard, by taking a personal interest, the chances for a sale will dramatically increase. These salespeople also reap the rewards of repeat sales, as they follow up with each and every customer in order to ensure complete satisfaction.

They stand behind their product, and, in fact, become larger than the product itself - at least in the eyes of the customer. These people-oriented salespeople are recognized as the authority in their respective fields. They are so highly regarded, that they are able to expand their customer base through the use of referrals. They are people that care about other people and get immense satisfaction in serving their fellow human beings.

Building Self-confidence

If you're to sell yourself successfully, you must have 100% confidence in yourself and your abilities. A lack of confidence is easily spotted by a prospect. It could be reflected in your voice or your hesitancy in answering a specific question. Self-confidence is something you have to work at on a daily basis as you can lose it.

The top sales-people have developed resilience in accepting defeat on occasion without taking the rejection as a personal affront. They maintain their self-confidence by getting off the floor and moving forward with greater resolve than ever before. Rather than brooding about the lost sale, they try to make the next sale as quickly as possible, thus reinforcing their belief that they are number one.

Make it a habit every day of ending the day on a high note by making a sale or appointment before you go home. Set the stage for a better tomorrow, by ending today on an upbeat note. It is a great exercise for building self-confidence and maintaining your momentum. Keep repeating that the world's greatest salesperson is YOU. Yes, YOU!

Focusing

Successful salespeople are winners because they are focused 100% on the task at hand. They are so intense on achieving their goals that they develop a tunnel vision of success. They follow a plan to the letter and never veer off track no matter what the odds or failure rate may be.

Consider the example of a client who is in the sales training business. This man has set a goal of making three new discoveries every day. In order to accomplish this objective a minimum of three new appointments must be secured on a daily basis. On some days it is necessary to make as many as 50 calls to get just three appointments. The client's role is to honour the appointment, make the discovery, write the proposal and ultimately to close the sale.

The primary objective is to get as many quality leads as is physically possible. Selling is a numbers game. The greater the numbers, the more closings you will have. It's as simple as that. If you want to be successful, it is necessary to pay the price. The price you pay is long, tedious hours of intense focusing, but the end result can be so rewarding.

As we talk about focusing, many readers might still remember how focused the great American high jumper, Dwight Stone, became before every jump. As he faced the bar, he mentally took every step in his approach preparation. As you watched his head nod up and down you could almost visualize him running and soaring over that bar.

That man was truly focused and it paid dividends. You too can develop your approach in the same manner, whether you are phone prospecting or making a presentation in person. Always focus on success, visualize the sale, assume the sale. Remove the word failure from your mind forever. You're the world's greatest salesman! Keep reinforcing it in your mind, 24 hours every day.

Persistence

The dictionary defines persistence as the act of persisting or the quality of being persistent. In the world of sales it means to never fold up the tent or give up without a fight. Persistence should not be associated with high pressure tactics or making a nuisance of oneself. Salespeople worth their salt have a persistent or insistent nature that can never be discouraged. They are emphatic in their request and are only satisfied when that request is satisfied.

Many prospects use trite objections to test your persistence to find out what you are really made of. If you lack an insistent nature in extolling the benefits that your product can offer, how do you think the prospect feels? If you're not fully committed to your product, the prospect certainly won't be and will not even permit you to make your presentation.

The other forms of persistence take place after the salesperson has made the presentation. The prospect is mildly interested in buying, but not now. Persistent salespeople will follow up on a regular basis, either by phone or in person to see if they can be of service.

Does this follow up system really work?

You bet it does! An innumerable number of sales have been closed ten or twelve months after the initial presentation was made. All those presentations would have been in vain, had it not been for a persistent follow-up program. The prospects that receive a follow up phone call, a personal visit or even a mailing periodically have got to be impressed.

They realize that you care, and that you have a follow up system in place. It indicates that you are highly organized, value their business, and as a result, could probably become a very reliable supplier to their firm.

The Smile of Fortune
Have you ever been in a room full of gloomy people and then watch a person enter that room with a big wide smile? The room all of a sudden lights up like a Christmas tree. It's as if that person with a smile is carrying a neon flashing sign with him.

A person who wears a smile is like the person that wears a sign on his back imploring you to eat at Joe's Deli. The major difference is that the smiling person doesn't need to wear a sign. His smile is a walking, talking advertisement that says I am a confident, happy, friendly, people-person who would like to get to know you. I am a nice person.

Change your attitude and smile. Your life will be richer for it.

Maintaining Sales Growth
Successful salespeople are consistently successful in maintaining high volume sales levels and incomes in both the good and the bad times. How do they possibly accomplish this? You might ask. The secret to their success is very simple. They never quit cold calling or prospecting. They never rest on their laurels. They realize that the more cold calls they make the more presentations they will be able to make. The more presentations that they make, the more sales they will close. It's still the numbers game, isn't it?

It all starts with a cost-efficient, high volume methodology which puts them into contact with as many prospects as possible - over the least amount of time. Years of consistent success have proven the viability of establishing appointments by phone. Through The Call Wizard you will learn their secret techniques. Inside salespeople will be able to carry these procedures further to actually close product sales as well.

Many successful people build their client base through the use of referrals from satisfied customers. They ask for and receive testimonial letters from both present and past customers. They sell themselves to new clients by using their success stories to full advantage.

The real sales leaders not only work harder, they work smarter. They become creative in their thinking and seek out and develop untapped secondary markets for their product line.

The top producers develop a systematic call-back cycle for their established accounts. They service these accounts in the same intense manner in which they originally secured the business. By so doing, they are always poised to sell additional product or to up sell when the customer need arises.

In summation, to keep the momentum going your way, never quit cold calling. Build your client base through the use of referrals, develop secondary markets and service the devil out of your existing customers.

Professional Development

The elite salespeople, no matter how successful they become, are consistently striving to improve their selling skills through ongoing training programs.

Just as professional baseball teams and hockey teams always go back to learning the basics in an effort to sharpen their skills, salespeople that are winners are habitually striving to improve themselves. They maintain an open mind to new ideas and selling methods and are willing to employ innovative new ideas wherever and whenever possible. Many career salespeople make it a point of taking a sales training course at least once a year. They listen to motivational CDs on the car stereo while travelling both to and from work and seek and read fresh new books on the selling profession.

The selling profession is such a complex one that no one individual knows all the answers. There is no such thing as the perfect salesperson. We all have weaknesses that have to be identified and corrected. If you hope to reach the top echelon of your profession you must be totally honest with yourself and admit that you could use help in specific areas of the sales process.

The secret to improvement in any field of endeavour is to work hard and turn your weaknesses into strengths. You should also strive to know your product inside and out and keep abreast of any and all new developments in your industry.

If you are a golf fan, you might remember watching a certain young and virtually unknown golfer win the PGA Championship. He hit the ball harder and farther than anyone in the history of the game. Even Jack Nicklaus, arguably the greatest golfer of all time, was in awe of this young man. Many thought that this young man's game would collapse and that he would eventually finish far back in the pack of what many considered one of the finest field of golfers ever assembled.

John Daly or Long John Daly - as he is affectionately known - did not fold, but rather got stronger and stronger as the tournament progressed and claimed his first major championship - the PGA title.

John Daly - prior to the PGA - wasn't a household word, and, in fact, had never threatened to win a tournament on the PGA circuit. You see, John had a weakness - a major weakness - in his game.

Although he was able to hit the ball out of sight, he really never knew where it was going to land. John Daly worked and worked at harnessing all that power and eventually turned his weakness into his major strength - the ability to hit the golf ball longer than anyone in the game and with deadly accuracy.

Discover your weaknesses, turn them into your strengths and climb to the pinnacle of sales success. You can do it, if you want it badly enough.

Contact Level Comfortability

The true sales professional learns to be humble in dealing with fellow human beings. This statement is not to infer that you should become submissive in nature, but rather that you express a sense of selflessness and modesty.

When it was suggested that YOU are the world's greatest salesperson, the intent was not for you to be going around telling people that you are the best salesperson in the world. It was meant solely for your own psyche, your own belief in yourself

In the sales profession, depending to some degree on the industry in which you are working, you will be dealing with people from all walks of life. One day, you could be making a presentation to the CEO of a major corporation while a few hours later, you could be dealing with a common labourer. It is even conceivable that you could be dealing with both levels on the social ladder at the same time.

If for example, you are selling maintenance equipment to a small company, you may be making your initial presentation to the maintenance mechanic. In all probability, your follow-up call may find you dealing with the president in order to secure the signing of a contract. The secret in dealing with people from different backgrounds and stature is to exhibit total respect for the opinions of each individual.

You must be able to converse intelligently at each level and to make each person feel like the most important person in the world at the time of your meeting.

Well-read salespeople are at a decided advantage as they have a grasp of many subjects and can adapt easily to any subject matter or situation.

Humble salespeople can adjust their social standing and conversation level to achieve compatibility with the people to whom they are speaking. It would not be prudent for example, if a salesperson began to talk like a rocket scientist to a prospect who only wants to know what benefits your equipment offers.

If, on the other hand, you are making the proposal to the chief engineer, a Harvard graduate, who wants to know precisely how your product functions, then, and only then will you, be able to make an impact with your rocket scientist impression. In order to achieve contact level comfort-ability, treat the person to whom you are speaking, as you yourself would like to be treated. Adjust your conversation level, within reason of course, to that of the other party.

Enthusiasm

A salesperson can have all qualities that have been mentioned in this profile; they can have all the self- confidence in the world; can be 100% focused; and yet, if enthusiasm lacks, they have nothing.

Many sales managers look for enthusiasm above all other characteristics when interviewing a prospective salesperson for their companies. Their thinking is that an enthusiastic person is more likely to accept direction and is more easily trained in company sales procedures and methodology than an unenthusiastic person.

You can sell anything, if you can sell yourself with enthusiasm.

Even if you are not a naturally enthusiastic person, you can become enthusiastic by training your thought process. Think about something that you look forward to doing in your spare time and mentally transfer it over to your next presentation. It could be a hobby, it could be a sport in which you like to participate, or it could even be that special vacation that you are planning for the near future.

Put a smile on your face and as you drive down the highway and repeat the following: I am enthusiastic and I will make everyone I meet today enthusiastic! It really works!

Product Knowledge

Last - but certainly not least in the profile section - is the acquiring of product knowledge. A good solid understanding of what your product does and how it functions will probably be adequate in dealing with 95% of your prospects.

What about the other 5%? Your ability to sell this remaining 5% of the market could mean the difference between becoming a good salesperson or a great salesperson. Great salespeople cultivate an extraordinary amount of product knowledge through self discovery and study.

It doesn't matter what product you sell or what service you offer, it is to your advantage to learn everything you possibly can learn. Associate yourself with the technical people in your company, and pick their brains for all the information that you can gather. Never stop asking questions about how your product is made or why certain procedures are used. Try to learn something new every day and you will succeed in selling that all important 5%.

Now that we have looked at a number of strengths and attributes that you must develop to be a successful person, it is only logical to consider to various personality types with whom you will be doing business.

You sometimes hear salespeople state that they are unable to deal with a buyer or a prospect because of a personality clash with the prospect. In some instances, if the prospect doesn't see things exactly the same way as the salesperson, the salesperson throws up his hands in despair and gives up.

The real sales pros have developed an ability to read the personality type of the person with whom they are dealing and to adjust their thought process to fit those of the prospect. By listening to and observing the prospect, the salespeople are able to get in sync with the other party.

They develop an almost uncanny ability to read the customer's mind, and, in fact, can predict what the customer's next question or statement will be, even before the prospect says it. Many people will say that this type of salesperson is a natural, born salesperson. That is pure bunk!

There is no such thing as a natural, born salesperson. The fact is, that this talent is acquired through many long hours of practice, trial and error, and experience.

Here is a system that will eliminate the trial and error approach, and that will dramatically increase your productivity levels. You must provide the experience and practice the system in order to make it work effectively for you.

Personality Types

There are four major personality types that you will have to identify and learn to deal with in the sales process. They are: The Entertainer, The Diplomat, The Sceptic and the Competitor. By listening and by observing, each type can be readily identified by how they express themselves verbally on the phone or in person. Through identification, you will learn how best to close them on either granting you an appointment or closing a sale.

The Entertainer

When The Entertainer greets you on the phone or in person, the greeting is usually friendly and warm. This personality type likes to hear a "How Are You Today?" greeting, and is most likely to return the same question to you. Entertainers are direct and to the point, yet tend to be open and talkative if the conversation or subject is stimulating in their mind's eye. They are enthusiastic and like to set a fast pace.

In dealing with Entertainers, take the time to listen what they have to say and wait until they wind down. Entertainers are creative in their thinking and welcome new ideas. Keep the conversation moving at a relatively fast pace. As Entertainers have a good sense of humour, inject a little fun into the conversation at the appropriate time.

Do not present a lot of facts, avoid being distant or aloof and remain flexible.

If Entertainers like you and the product or service you are offering, the sale or appointment can be closed right away - providing that you can deliver what you promise.

The Diplomat

This particular personality is also a friendly caring type who will listen to your complete sales presentation without interruption. Diplomats dislike any semblance of conflict and are likely to be agreeable with you. Don't be misled, however; as Diplomats are slow decision makers who avoid taking any risks. They are non-assertive and will try putting off the decision to meet with you until they talk with other personnel within their company.

When making a presentation to Diplomats, it is very important to leave them with the impression that you sincerely care about their problems and value their input. When speaking, remain relaxed and informal. Always assure Diplomats that the risk factor in dealing with you is virtually non-existent. Always reiterate that any details that you are, or will be presenting to them will be put in writing.

Do not get overly aggressive or try to force them to make a decision. Do not avoid questions by dismissing them as being insignificant.

In closing the sale or appointment, stress ongoing support, follow up and any other assurance which may be necessary.

The Sceptic

The Sceptic is a cool and aloof type of individual whose voice lacks any real warmth. Sceptics are generally, unlikely to be open with strangers. They will usually be very up front with you in indicating their scepticism. This personality type has an analytical mind that will test both your patience and you mettle by demanding detailed answers to what are sometimes very complicated questions. For this reason, make sure you know your subject matter inside out.

Sceptics are most likely to ask for references in order to ease their own doubts about your company's background and it's abilities to serve their needs. They are great procrastinators, who will, sometimes, resort to the tritest excuses in order to delay the buying decision.

In dealing with Sceptics, avoid using the latest buzz words, refrain from the use of light-hearted small talk and don't exert too much pressure for an immediate decision.

In order to secure the appointment or sale, take a logical, organized approach in your presentation and provide totally accurate and honest answers to any and all questions. Ask for the appointment or sale in a low key manner and agree to provide detailed information in writing.

The Competitor

Competitors are impatient individuals, who are very likely to use only their last name when answering the phone. They do not welcome small talk, so don't bother asking how they feel. Competitors like people who are fast paced like themselves and who are productive. They are, indeed competitive in every way, and focused on successful results.

Competitors shoot from the hip, are impatient and want immediate action and results. They make independent decisions, are very strong willed and hate to lose. They want also to be assured that you will not waste their valuable time. If you have asked for five minutes or fifteen minutes of their valuable time, you can bet that when your time allocation has expired, you will be unceremoniously advised that the presentation is finished - even if it is not.

Competitors like to control every situation, so let them think that they are in control.

When going for the close, give concise, specific information in a forthright, hard hitting manner. Always give Competitors several options after asking for the order, as they will definitely balk if they feel that their back is to the wall.

You have been given an overview of the four major personality types that you will be encountering on a daily basis. Following is an exercise to complete that is intended to help you retain what you have read. You will find 14 characteristics listed under the heading: Personality Types. Place five characteristics into each of the four personality categories where you think that they will best fit.

It should be noted that some of the characteristics may apply to more than one personality style. CHOOSE THE ONE WHERE IT FITS MOST STRONGLY.

Personality Types

THE ENTERTAINER

THE DIPLOMAT

THE SKEPTIC

THE COMPETITOR

Characteristics

(a)   good sense of humour good listener

(b)   tells you what you want to hear

(c)   likes to exercise control over others

(d)   open and talkative demands immediate action and results

(e)   avoids risk

(f)   full of enthusiasm cool and aloof

(g)   impatient

(h)   very strong willed creative

(i)   analytical

(j)   believes in a logical approach

(k)   firm decision maker dislikes and avoids conflict

(l)   a great procrastinator

(m)   friendly and warm personality

(n)   slow decision maker likes lots of detail

How many did you get correct?

Following are the correct placements:

THE ENTERTAINER:
friendly and warm
open and talkative
full of enthusiasm
good sense of humour
creative

THE DIPLOMAT:
good listener
dislikes or avoids conflicts
tells you what you want to hear
slow decision maker
avoids risks

THE SKEPTIC:
cool and aloof
analytical
likes lots of detail
believes in a logical approach
great procrastinator

THE COMPETITOR:
likes to exercise
control over others
firm decision maker
demand immediate action and results
very strong willed impatient

What Personality Type Are You?

Go back and review the four major personality types, and determine which, of the four, best fits yourself. Keep in mind that we all have characteristics from every category that surface at one time or another, however; most of us are dominant in a specific personality type.

There is no right or wrong type for sales people. The main objective in determining personality type is to help you develop an instant strategy that will help you get positive results.

Now let's look at the strengths, the weaknesses and the areas needing improvement in each style from a salesperson's perspective.

Personality Style: Strengths. Weaknesses and Areas Needing Improvement

The Entertainer Salesperson

The Entertainer salespeople excel at sales meetings due to their expressive nature and feel right at home in writing proposals where they can let their creative juices run free.

On the negative side, Entertainers are least comfortable with planning and providing assurances. In order to improve, they must discipline themselves to become better organized. In order to accomplish this goal, they should develop a questionnaire and an accompanying check list to ensure success.

The Diplomat Salesperson: Strengths and Weaknesses

These sales types are very introspective. Their strengths include assuring skills, and an above average ability to study and analyze needs.

Improvement, however, is needed in the area of problem solving skills. Diplomats - naturally friendly people - can also improve their sales career by focusing first and foremost on helping others. By so doing, they will enhance their own potential for increased opportunities.

The Sceptic Salesperson: Strengths and Weaknesses

The natural propensity for detail makes Sceptics ideally suited to the planning and studying process. They are, however; somewhat lacking at the meeting stage and need to work consistently on closing techniques.

Sceptics, while able to develop new ideas, must focus on developing skills that will enable them to implement these new ideas. Sceptics - somewhat aloof and withdrawn - must work at developing relationships and becoming more people oriented and friendly towards others.

The Competitor Salesperson: Strengths and Weaknesses

Competitors, fast paced and goal oriented, know what they want and how to get it. Outstanding planners, they know how to close sales and are able to achieve any goal through determination and strong will power.

Competitors have a major weakness. This is impatience with the planning and analyzing process. Improvement in these areas is achievable if they learn to slow down, relax and listen more intently to clients' needs.

The Entertainer

Strengths

- develops creative proposals

- strong presentation skills

Weaknesses

- proper planning

- providing assurances

Areas of improvement

- better organization of details

- create a check list

-

The Diplomat Strengths

- analyzing abilities

- providing assurances

Weaknesses

- the proposal

- closing skills

Areas of improvement

- focus on problem solving

- become more assertive

-

The Sceptic Strengths

- planning

- studying

Weaknesses

-       meeting skills

-       closing skills

Areas of improvement

-       improve relationships

-       put ideas into effect

-

The Competitor Strengths

-       planning

-       closing

Weaknesses

-       studying

-       assuring

Areas of improvement

-       slow down

-       spend more time with client

When selling the various personality types, there are specific presentation and closing skills that should be emphasized in order to bring about a successful conclusion.

The Sceptic Presentation tips

-       provide detailed information

-       provide guarantees to minimize risk

-       be clear and precise

-       be business like

Closing tips

-       ask for order in low key manner

-       be prepared to negotiate

- put proposal in writing

- combat stalling with guarantees, test markets etc.

-

The Competitor Presentation tips

- be brief and to the point

- provide specific information

- let the competitor think he has control

- be strictly business-like

Closing tips

- overcome stalling by repeating strongest benefits

- offer options

- be prepared to negotiate your proposal

- ask directly for the order

-

The Diplomat Presentation tips

- present information in writing

- build a personal relationship

- be informal

- minimize the risks with guarantees

Closing tips

- provide assurances that you will follow up personally

- overcome stalling by alleviating personal concerns

- offer to put agreement in writing

- ask for the order indirectly

-

The Entertainer Presentation tips

-        ask for their opinions and encourage input

-        build a personal relationship

-        be expressive and stimulating

-        move rapidly

-        show a sense of humour

Closing tips

-        sell the main benefits

-        offer to look after all the details

-        avoid buying hesitation by offering special incentives

-        close on the spot

-        get the order in writing

The Impersonation Factor

The dictionary defines the verb impersonate as the ability to act or play the part of

In Sales, you must be able to play the role of each of the personality types with whom you will be dealing with on a regular basis. At the same time, you must never lose sight of who you are.

As you become an all round actor, you will be better able to deal with every personality type with equal ease and confidence. All it takes is practice and more practice.

One very effective exercise is to practice on your family and friends in determining individual personality types. Keep it light hearted, high spirited and full of fun. You'll be surprised at how interested and keen the participants will become as their personality types become evident.

II.   SETTING PERSONAL GOALS

Every successful athlete or business person has achieved success through a series of planned goal setting objectives. It is fine to have all the natural ability in the world, along with drive and determination, but without a realistic goal or objective, all of these attributes become meaningless. People without specific goals find themselves running helter-skelter in all direction.

They are bereft of any logical goals and always complain of constantly running into stiff head winds. When asked if they have a goal, the reply is typically that they are going to be successful and make a lot of money. "What is wrong with that sort of goal? You might ask.

Nothing is wrong with that statement, except that it is too vague and does not focus on specific goals. And what is wrong with making a little amount of money before making a lot of money.

People endeavouring to turn the world upside down and become overnight success stories are generally the ones that are always trying to hit the home run every time they go to bat. The home run hitters of the business world generally become the strikeout kings and are soon forgotten- never to be heard from again. They have failed to develop a sound base, on which to build their business.

It is the singles hitters of the world that are the real winners because of their planned approach. Their initial goal is to reach first base. They are aware that by constantly hitting those singles, the runs or personal goals will take care of themselves.

Speaking of goals, how about Brett, The Golden Brett, Hull of the National Hockey League who is now retired. He scored 86 goals in his first season for St. Louis, the first NHL team to give him an opportunity to play on a full time basis. Every year since that initial season, Brett filled opposition nets with goals, and became one of the most prolific goal scorer in hockey history.

When asked how he accomplished such enormous goal scoring numbers, Brett admitted that he really didn't know, and that he did not set goal scoring quotas for himself at the beginning of each season. Hull did reveal, however, that his aim was to score as many goals as possible in every game that he played. The golden one - as he was affectionately known - believed in taking one game at a time and that the numbers would be there at the end of the season. They were indeed!

He set one game objectives for long term results. It is interesting to note that Brett Hull usually took more shots on the net than any other NHL player. Remember the numbers game we mentioned earlier?

You can be the Golden Brett of your sales team if you just apply some basic principles and establish a blueprint for success. Here is the secret blueprint: Follow it religiously, believe in it, use it wisely and keep it updated on a daily basis.

The first step in this unique blueprint plan is to set up a personal goals chart for yourself. Don't use or mention dollars in your objectives, but rather use terms such as sales units or contracts. Your number one priority is the achievement of x number of appointments and sales units.

If you achieve these sales unit objectives, the dollars will follow. Use your blueprint to chart daily and weekly progress. At the end of each week develop a fresh blueprint for the next week. Set realistic goals for yourself. Any and all objectives should be achievable targets and yet should not be set so high that they are impossible to achieve.

Following is the chart example:

January - Week # 1 to January 1st - 5th

	MON	TUES	WED	THURS	FRI
Target # of appointments.					
Cumulative					
# of actual appointments.					
Cumulative					
Target # of units sold					
Cumulative					
# of actual units sold					
Cumulative					

In addition to the daily and weekly chart, set up monthly charts in order to track your progress. By so doing, you will be better able to pinpoint your weaknesses and build on your strengths. Selling is a numbers game, that is, the more presentations that you make, the greater the number of closings you will achieve. The key is to build up your appointment count in order to make those extra presentations.

Although every industry or field of endeavour is different, statistics indicate that an average sales person will close one of every five presentations given. If you are relatively inexperienced in the sales field, it could take ten presentations to achieve one sale. Don't be discouraged.

Your success rate will surge upward as you become more adept and comfortable with the sales process and with your product offering. Keep practicing your sales techniques and you will soon join the ranks of the elite sales professionals who close one out of every three prospects.

Thus far, we have concentrated on sales units rather than dollar sales. Let's take a look at an example of how the number of sales units translates into dollars and how the closing ratio can effect income levels. Let's assume that you generate a commission of $250.00 per sales unit. If it takes you an average of five presentations in one day to make one sale, you will have earned $250.00 for that day.

That translates into $50.00 for each presentation given. If you sell for 250 days of the year, your income will be $62,500.00. You will, in fact, have made 1250 actual presentations to achieve that same income level.

Assuming that you have improved your professional sales expertise, and that your sales presentation skills have been refined and improved after the first 12 months, let's look at what can be achieved if you can secure a sale for every three presentations rather than every five presentations. Based on the same number of annual presentations - 1250 - you will now close 417 sales versus 250, in the previous year.

Your new closing ratio will now reflect an income of $250.00 x 417 = $104,250.00 - an increase of better than 60% in annual earnings. This increase came about as a direct result of improving your selling skills. You, in fact, worked smarter not harder, and achieved dramatic sales volume increases. Amazing isn't it! What would happen if you worked harder and smarter at the same time? The results are simply staggering.

As an example, if you were to make just one more appointment and one more presentation each day, your total presentations would increase from 1250 to 1500 per annum. Based on a one in three closing ratio, you would secure 500 sales over the next twelve months. Your total yearly income would then escalate to $125,000.00.

Determine what income level you would like to achieve and work back the numbers for your daily and weekly blueprint chart. Plan your own success and successfully implement the plan. Be focused every day, every week, every month, and you will achieve all your objectives. Your only limitations are those that you place on yourself. Go for it NOW!

How to develop a Market Focus

The next logical step in the planning process is to determine your prime target market - the types of customers to whom you primarily want to direct your marketing efforts. If you are engaged in the manufacturing sector, as an example, it would be wise to direct your initial thrust towards those industries that you feel are most likely to use your services.

Caution should be exercised at all times, however, when you are going through this selection stage. Although a specific industry may appear to be a perfect fit for your product line or service, it is conceivable that this particular industry could be in a severe economic downturn.

Although this industry may see the obvious benefits of your service, it may very well not generally be able to afford your services.

As you want to build your customer base as quickly as possible, you would be wise to seek out industries that are relatively healthy and are more able to afford your product or service.

Prime Target Markets

It is important to prioritize the types of industry, or consumers, in order of importance to the success of your business as you see it. Your order of importance may later be have to be altered, but, at least you are developing a prime prospect list. The most important target market list could be labelled as the A Prospects, the second most important, the B Prospects, and the least important, the C Prospects.

It is critical that you never prejudge any business prospect, no matter how small or insignificant that particular business may appear to be. That small business that you ignore could very well be a subsidiary of a huge conglomerate that offers unlimited opportunities for your company.

Secondary Markets

Many companies become so obsessed with their market niche that they completely ignore the all important secondary market potential. This secondary market, in many cases, generates enough income to cover all overhead costs, and in recessional times it can provide the means by which a company can survive a significant downturn in their primary business.

The development of a secondary market requires a fertile imagination on the part of the management and the company's sales team. Secondary markets are there for the taking if you remain alert and develop an ability to feel the pulse of the real world around you. Following is a specific example of how the development of a secondary market saved one company from certain bankruptcy.

The company involved was a major player in the plastics industry. They had developed an impeccable and enviable reputation in the development of proto-types for the aerospace and automotive industries. During their heyday in the 1980's much of their business was referral business. The dollar volume levels and accompanying profits showed double digit increases through almost a decade.

Then the unthinkable happened - a deep and lasting recession. The good times were over as the economy ground to a halt.

Unfortunately, the sales people in this organization had forgotten how to sell. They had, in fact, become glorified order takers. The future looked very bleak indeed.

It was during a brainstorming management meeting that a hidden source of revenue was staring them right in the face. The plant manager, in showing actual samples of past work that had been produced for a number of clients, casually handed a plastic stand up desk calendar to a business consultant.

The calendar on the one side showed the months of the current year while the calendar on the opposite side detailed all dates for the next year. When asked if they could customize these calendars for individual companies, the plant manager responded positively and stated that they had the stamping capabilities to produce any quantity at any time.

At that very instant, the lights went on in the consultant's head. This simple little desk calendar would be the saviour of the company. A gold mine had been uncovered. When it was explained to management that this simple little calendar was one of the best sales promotion products seen for a long time, they suddenly awoke from their collective coma.

As strange as this story may seem to you, it is nevertheless true, and in fact, reflects a common malady that is commonplace in North America industry today. Small to medium sized companies become so focused on developing their market niche that they are oblivious to development of vital secondary markets.

The first order of business was to develop several phone scripts that would help achieve market penetration in the sales promotion area. The main theme to be portrayed was that the company had a hot item - along with several others - that would virtually assure that any client selling a product or service would be remembered long after the actual presentation had been made.

This durable plastic calendar had a life cycle of two years. It was stressed that every time a client's prospect picked up the phone, the prospect would be looking at that company's name that was imprinted on the calendar. Most important, it was emphasized that unlike pens or other sales promotion items that are used and discarded or, in fact, completely misplaced or lost, this unique calendar remained stationary for two full years.

Due to its composition, it could be handled on a daily basis without ever becoming soiled or frayed. It was an indestructible as well as an indispensable business item. Could anyone find a more cost effective means of advertising?

The second series of phone scripts were aimed at any company that already had a captive market and was not really sales oriented. The emphasis here was on the company's developmental expertise, its flexibility, and the proven ability to produce literally anything made of plastic, from the proto-type stage through to large volume production runs.

The short term strategy was to secure enough business in the specialized sales promotion area in order to get the plant operational once again and to cover overhead costs.

The long term objective was to revitalize the prototype business and to combine it with an ever increasing sales promotion business to produce a balanced source of income. This is precisely what occurred. As doors were opened with the sales promotion or advertising specialty line, other doors from within the companies with whom they were doing business also opened.

The sales people discovered that cross selling was not only possible, but that it was expected of them on each every call. After the easy sell in the specialty advertising field, each representative would ask to be introduced to the plant manager or engineering department. It was in this area that the real selling began. As the number of seeds planted grew and grew over a period of months, so grew the number of production orders.

The advertising specialty business also expanded in leaps and bounds, and in fact, mushroomed to the point where prospects were actually phoning the office to request a visit from a representative.

The turnaround took less than one year - proof positive that with a little imagination and a lot of hard work, success can be yours, if you want it badly enough.

Whether you are an individual who has struck out on your own - or whether your company is small or large - the opportunities are out there in the so called secondary markets. Learn to value and respect your employee's opinions. Encourage think tank sessions to get fresh new ideas and don't dismiss any suggestions that are innovative in nature.

Group management participation is the wave of the future. The old philosophy of the boss - employee relationship is changing before our very eyes. The future will demand that all employees be equally as responsible as their superiors for the success or failure of their company. Management personnel, on the other hand, must learn to LISTEN to their subordinates and be prepared to share the profits when an outstanding idea bears fruit.

The Promotional Concept Account as it Relates to Secondary Markets

In the majority of instances, the promotional concept idea applies to or can be sold to those businesses that sell high ticket or costly items as well as those companies that sell extremely high volumes of product. There are dozens of examples as to how you could cash-in on the promotional concept idea. Following are several examples:

You're in the publishing business and are launching a book on cross-country skiing. Why not go to a major manufacturer of cross-country skis with a proposal that he gives away a free copy of the book with every pair of skis purchased. Simply brilliant, don't you think? Not really, it's just a matter of using your imagination.

How about an appliance dealer giving out a voucher for X dollars worth of beef for every freezer ordered during a specific time period. A high profile or quality home builder giving away a free cellular phone with every home purchased.

There isn't a business out there that can't be tied-in directly to the consumer or to another business. Think about it for a minute! When the going gets tough, get innovative:

Although the ideas for the promotional concept marketing of your product line may be endless, it must be remembered that it is still up to you to sell that concept. In developing your presentation for a promotional concept prospect it is of paramount importance that you meet certain criteria in both your written and verbal offering. The following points should be highlighted and emphasized:

- You are offering a fresh new approach

- Your promotional idea will be unique in your prospect's industry

- You have a product that everyone wants and needs (back up this statement with statistics)

- You will unconditionally guarantee your product

- Your prospect's customers will remember the company every time they use the product

- Your concept - if handled with expertise - will prove to be a cost effective way to achieve dramatic sales volume increases

Following is a sample written presentation made on behalf of a cellular phone company a number of years ago to a major home builder. The builder did buy the concept and it ultimately became the greatest buyer incentive program in that particular company's history.

Are you looking for a refreshing and innovative approach in promoting your homes to people across this country?

Are you looking for that special idea in order to establish uniqueness that will separate your company from your competition?

The smallest difference in how you promote your company could be the most important difference.

We have the product of the new millennium. We are confident that our product, combined with your marketing expertise, will prove to be the most successful buyer incentive program of all time - at a reasonable cost.'

Our product is:

- a status symbol.

- a necessary tool for the new millennium.

- a profit and productivity booster

- *OUR PRODUCT IS A PORTABLE CELLULAR PHONE!*

In a recent business article that appeared in a major daily newspaper, it was estimated the cellular phone business will experience a 1200% growth rate over the next ten (10) years.

As the number one manufacturer of cellular phones in North America, we will guarantee your customers' satisfaction, backed by our three (3) year parts and labour warranty.

You will be remembered every time your customer uses his phone, you will be innovative and you will be believed.

We have designed a program exclusively for your use and would be highly honoured to serve you. We would be equally as honoured to be remembered as having played a small role in the development of the most successful Sales Incentive Program in your history.

Good Selling

Now develop your own presentation in your own words to fit your specific product line. Employ a dramatic flare in writing your proposal, but be careful not to be misleading. Write with sincerity and enthusiasm and always be prepared to reinforce statistics with documented evidence.

Follow-up your written proposal with a phone call to secure an appointment to close the sale. Condense the contents of your proposal into an effective 30 second script.

The business is out there, just waiting to be had, but you have to pursue it with vigor and determination. Knock on enough doors and you will get your fair share of that all important secondary market business.

Assignment:
Develop two or three phone scripts on the preceding written proposal. Critique your offering after studying Chapter III, Developing A Script.

Developing a Prospect List or Database

One of the best sources for obtaining prospect lists is through the Internet, local municipal government offices or Chambers of Commerce. Usually, the directories that are available, are updated on an annual basis and contain valuable information such as name and title of top executive contacts, e-mail addresses, telephone numbers, description of type of business, number of employees and fax numbers.

In addition to the directories published by local Chambers of Commerce, there are a number of other publications such as the Scott's or Might's directories that supply businesses with thousands of new sales prospects. If you are not initially willing to invest in the purchase of volumes and volumes of these directories, go to your local library and make photocopies of listings as required.

One additional source that should not be overlooked are those companies that specialize in routing services or direct mail. The industrial directories that they publish provide listings of manufacturers, wholesalers, distributors, importers and exporters, head offices of retail chains, and service companies such as printers, contractors etc.

The routing companies can provide you with a competitive edge as they continually update their lists throughout the year. As a result, you will be able to target your market more efficiently. Routing service companies usually divide large metropolitan cities into dozens of marketing areas.

This breakdown allows you to develop a grid, for your marketing area and ensures that you will be able to plan your coverage in the most cost effective and efficient manner possible.

Routing service companies are also able to provide professional directories that lists thousands of firms and individuals in at least a couple of hundred categories including accountants, architects, engineers, insurance companies, legal firms and lawyers, consultants, medical doctors, real estate companies ... and many more.

An often overlooked source of excellent prospect leads can be found in the help wanted section of local and major newspapers, specialized employment publications as well as on popular employment websites.

Any company that is hiring new personnel is making a statement that it is a progressive organization that is poised for expansion. Capitalize on this information on a daily basis and you will gain the competitive edge.

Establishing the Proper Contact Level

Now that you have compiled a prospect list, it is up to you to use that list to your full advantage by determining the correct contact level at which to direct your phone presentation.

Many of your listings will show the name of the president, the general manager, the plant manager or sales manager. To whom do you ask to speak? Having worked with a great number of sales people over the years, it may or may not surprise you that the vast majority of people ask for anyone BUT the president. Why? Because they are afraid to start at the top.

These people are intimidated by the title and lack the confidence to go to the top executive or decision maker. They are gripped by the fear of failure and become paralysed at the thought of even speaking to an authority figure.

You must get over this fear immediately or you are doomed to failure. You must develop enough confidence in yourself, your product or service, and your ability to communicate, that addressing yourself to the top management level becomes second nature.

If you have a mental block when it comes to speaking at the presidential level, try this simple exercise. Write the name of the prospective company on your call back sheet. Beside the company name, write the name of the contact person. Do not write down that person's title. Now insert this sheet with your other follow up sheets or in your contact management database.

As your follow up calls will find you speaking to people from all management levels you will treat the name - that you set aside - as just another name and will be able to speak to that person as easily as you speak to your favourite Aunt Gertrude.

This unique method yields simply amazing results. As you gain confidence, you can abandon this habit or crutch as you will become fearless in your approach.

Always remember that it is easier to start at the top management level and work your way down, than it is to work from the bottom upwards. It is of critical importance to deal with top level management for the following reasons:

- Presidents of progressive companies like to be kept abreast of new product developments and/or services that are available to them.

- Most top executives admire people who have the gumption to talk directly to them.

- They are constantly striving to turn weak spots in their company into pillars of strength and are at least willing to listen to any proposal that will accomplish this objective.

- If the CEO likes what you have to offer he will tell you up front and will direct you to the correct contact level. In many instances, the CEO may want to meet directly with you.

- Once you have made it known to one of the president's subordinates that you were referred by the president, you will get a hearing every time.

There are other important reasons for dealing at the top executive level. Many department managers who have been in the same position for a number of years become complacent and, do not welcome change; in fact, they are fearful of any change, period. Others have developed a friendship with suppliers that they do not want to jeopardize, even if another company can offer a better product at a lower price.

Although your product or service may seem to dictate that you contact a specific person in middle management, be very cautious, as you could be very well be lead down a dead end street by that person.

Consider the lesson learned by the sales training consultant.

During the start up phase, all prospect calls were directed at sales managers. Most of the calls were met with rejection.

The reason for the negative response was very simple. Sales managers felt threatened by this outside expert who quite possibly would uncover their shortcomings.

The correct contact for this consultant was at the presidential level. Presidents are aware of both the strengths and weaknesses of their companies and are dedicated to converting the weak areas into pillars of strength.

In summation, reaching the ultimate decision maker takes a degree of courage and patience, but it is the most cost- effective and logical path to follow if you are to be successful.

In a later chapter you will learn exactly how to get past the secretary or receptionist in order to reach that key decision maker.

III.   DEVELOPING A SCRIPT

Just as the director of a theatrical production has to plan and synchronize every line in a stage play in order to create maximum impact on the audience, so do you have to plan your mini production.

As you won't be seen initially by your audience, it is critical that you create such a strong verbal image of yourself and your service that your sales prospect will want to see you immediately. You will have a maximum of 30 seconds to get the desired response. It doesn't matter what business you are involved with or what kind of track record you have had in the past with cold calls.

If you follow these methods exactly as outlined, you cannot and you will not fail. This system has been used with amazing success in virtually every field of endeavour, including the setting of appointments, market surveys, recruiting personnel, the selling of goods or services and even in the search for employment.

An effective script should outline your company's unique strengths, and should state exactly what your company does - the service that it provides, or the products that you sell. A good script must succinctly outline the problems that you solve, as well as your market focus.

Phone expertise is the foundation upon which most strong customer bases are built. Therefore, we will devote an extraordinary amount of time and space to this vital function. For most sales people - from the novice to the most seasoned professional - selling by phone as it relates to the cold call is the most intimidating experience one can imagine.

You don't believe it? Just look around the office and observe how hesitant your fellow sales reps are about calling prospective new accounts. They would rather drink coffee, eat donuts, or give themselves a manicure - anything but pick up that phone and make the first cold call. It really doesn't have to be this way if you take a logical, planned approach.

The first step towards a more positive attitude and enthusiast approach must come from your most inner thoughts.

Let's complete the following exercises before we proceed any further.

List what you expect from this section on script writing techniques. (Specific problems, fears etc.)

1.

2.

3.

4.

5.

6.

Prioritize the list above according to importance

1.

2.

3.

4.

5.

6.

Your company's unique strengths

1.

2.

3.

4.

5.

6.

Let's get on with the writing of a script that will open doors and create opportunities that you never imagined possible. Please read the guidelines that follow prior to writing your practice script:

- State who you are (Your name and company name)

- Your area of expertise (less than six words)

- Your company's specialty or focus

- State exactly what you do. The problems you solve.

- Ask for the appointment

My Phone Statement or Offering

Now read your script to your peers and get their honest reaction. Have them read the script to you. Be kind to one another and stress the positive aspects of each script first. Ask each other how each script could be improved. Now, read your script to a friend who knows little about your business.

Ask yourself the following questions:

Were you able to complete the reading of your script within the 30 second time period?

Any script that lasts longer than 30 seconds loses its impact. You must remember that people are inundated with calls every day and simply don't have the time or patience to listen to a rambling oration.

Did you get the prospects undivided attention?

Did the prospect understand fully what you do? Did you use a "hook"?

What is a "hook"? you might ask. A hook is a method of making a strong statement in the form of a question. It encourages a positive response. In fact, if a hook is worded correctly, it is virtually impossible for a prospect to say no without appearing to be an idiot. You will be given a number of examples of the hook method in the sample scripts.

Did you use Power Words?

The following power words reflect confidence and results:

Unique	Comprehensive
Creative	Increase
Dramatic	Versatile
Full Service	Solve
Cost Efficient	Get Together
Strategic	Agreement
Solution-Oriented	Opportunity
Success	Bottom-line

Always avoid words that have a negative connotation such as: buy it, deal, contract, set appointment.

Assignment:

In Chapter II, under Secondary Markets, you were asked to write a script based on a written presentation for your specific product line or service. Refer back to that script and revise it to conform to the guidelines that you have just been given. A third revision may be advisable after you have completed this section on script writing. Perfection can only be achieved by doing ordinary things extraordinarily well.

Let us now take a look at a number of sample scripts in a number of different industries. Study each one carefully and design your own scripts around the best of these sample scripts.

Do not deviate from the main structural layout of the scripts that you are about to read. The format used has been proven to be successful on thousands upon thousands of calls. As mentioned earlier in the book, it is critical that you discipline yourself to feeling comfortable with these methods. They are so simple and yet so very effective.

Sample Scripts:

Sample Sales Script #1: A Lift Truck Company

Scenario: You are talking to the president of the company with the intention of selling lift trucks.

> Good morning Mr./Mrs.   My name is   I'm with ABC Canada - The Materials Handling People.
>
> You don't know me, so I'll be brief! Is that okay?
>
> ABC Canada specializes in improving the cost efficiency and flexibility of materials handling requirements. We have experience in a wide variety of industries.
>
> I have only one question to ask you:
>
> If we could significantly lower your operating costs and dramatically increase your profitability, could we have 15 minutes of your time?
>
> (Wait for the response)
>
> Are mornings or afternoons best for you?
>
> MAKE THE APPOINTMENT

An alternative to the question or hook illustrated in this example could be as follows: If we could raise your profits and lower your costs, could we have 15 minutes of your time?

Let's briefly analyze why this type of script is so effective. First and foremost, it is concise and to the point. The statement I'll be brief, is that okay? gets prospects involved immediately and evokes a positive response before they even know what you are going to say.

You have captured their attention; you have asked for and received their permission to speak; and most important, you have shown that you respect the time that will be allocated to you.

Take a minute to think about what has just been stated. You, a complete stranger to a certain prospect have just disrupted the busy work schedule of a chief executive officer with an unsolicited phone call. With a few carefully chosen, simple words followed by a request for attention in the form of a question, you have brought the personal business of a company president to a grinding halt.

This point is not made to put you on an ego trip, but rather to emphasize how far you've progressed in a matter of two or three seconds. That's powerful stuff when you think about it! Now you have the responsibility of holding up to your end of the bargain.

The first script clearly identifies your specialty and mentions the benefits in broad strokes that can be expected. It uses power words such as cost efficiency, flexibility, dramatically, profitability, all to good advantage. The close in the form of a question, effectively uses the hook to secure a meeting.

The last statement: Are mornings or afternoons best for you? illustrates that you are entirely flexible and respect the prospect's busy schedule. Most important, you have shifted the prospect's attention away from the business at hand to concentrating solely on when the prospect is available.

The prospect is now at the point of no return and is committed to turning that yes response into a concrete meeting.

Let's take a look at a second script for that same lift truck company. This time however, you want to sell a customer service plan or maintenance program to the maintenance supervisor.

Good morning Mr./Mrs. ………… My name is ………… I'm with ABC Canada - The Materials Handling Co.

I'll just take a moment of your time. Is that okay?

Our Company has recently expanded our parts and service department quite substantially. We are introducing a new customer service plan that covers virtually all makes and models of lift equipment.

Just one question:

If we could show you, exactly, how to realize substantial savings on your normal maintenance costs, could we have 15 minutes of your time?

or the alternative hook

If we could raise your uptime, and lower downtime, could we have 15 minutes of your time? (Wait for the response)

Are mornings or afternoons best for you?

Producing A Script: Common Mistakes To Avoid

Thus far, you have practiced writing your own scripts and have read a couple of sample scripts that have proven to be highly successful.

Let's take a look at another version of a script that was developed by another salesperson for the same lift truck company.

Good Morning Mr./Mrs. ………… My name is ………… I'm with ABC Canada - The Materials Handling Co. Are you busy right now?

ABC specializes in narrow aisle lift trucks and order pickers. We also have an extensive line of walking and rider type pallet trucks and electric lift trucks that could make your business more efficient.

We have just developed a new automated guide vehicle that I think you will find to be a real breakthrough.

We will look at your warehouse and the inefficiencies that exist and make recommendations to improve your operation. We would like to set up an appointment to review our entire product line. In this way, we can determine whether or not we can help you. I am planning to be in your area anyway on and would you like to arrange a meeting with you in the early afternoon if that's all right with you.

Now it's your turn to be the judge. What is wrong with this script and why? Stop reading right now and study the last script again. List on a sheet of paper the things that you feel are wrong with this script. It has been written by a fairly successful sales representative who has a great deal of technical knowledge. This sales rep, however, has had very little success in generating new prospects through cold calling efforts.

Let's Now Compare Notes:

Mistake #1
The salesperson asked if the prospect was busy. Even if the prospect was not, do you think the prospect would admit it? Of course not!

Mistake #2
The salesperson had verbal diarrhoea (pardon the expression) and was inundating the prospect with product information that the prospect might not even be able to use. The script was far too lengthy and time consuming.

Mistake #3
The salesperson mentioned setting an appointment. This terminology sounds too committal and too demanding and final. It can have an intimidating connotation.

Mistake #4

By mentioning inefficiencies, the sales person is implying that the prospect runs an inefficient operation. How do you think the prospect feels towards this stranger?

Mistake #5

By mentioning that the salesperson will be in the prospect's area anyway, indicates that the salesperson is doing the prospect a big favour by dropping in to see them. This attitude indicates that the salesperson is not really concerned enough about the prospect to justify a special trip.

Mistake #6

The salesperson did not employ the hook in order to get a firm commitment.

Summary:

This salesperson would have been terminated by the prospect after the first or second mistake. The door to the office of this prospect would be closed up tight. Do you see the errors of this salesperson's methods? And yet, most salespeople keep committing the same errors day in and day out. They truly cannot understand why they are being constantly rejected.

Let's now change directions and look at how to sell an intangible service over the phone. The next sample script was specifically designed to promote a sales training company. This particular company works with groups or individuals who wish to improve their selling skills.

This particular script was produced from a five page document that had been used for direct mailing purposes. The entire message has been condensed into a dynamic 30 second phone commercial. Again, let's presume that we are addressing our phone presentation to the president of a medium sized company with 6 or so sales representatives.

Sample Sales Script #2: A Sales Training Company

Good morning Mr. Mrs. ………… My name is ………… I'm with Dynamo International - the sales development people.

I'll be very brief Is that alright?

Dynamo International offers a unique sales development program that maximizes sales results through specific direction and support. I have just one question to ask you:

If we could help your company to achieve dramatic sales volume increases could we have 15 minutes of your time?

(Wait for the response)

Are mornings or afternoons best for you?

MAKE THE APPOINTMENT

This script is truly a classic. It identifies who you are, what you do, gives benefits and uses the hook to achieve a positive response. It is brief, yet power packed with information that allows you to go for the jugular in an amiable manner. This script has been used to secure thousands of appointments and has received almost an equal number of compliments on its effectiveness.

The most common response that you will receive from a prospect is a hearty laugh and the following comment: I'd be fool to say no to a question like that, wouldn't I. You quickly agree when a prospect makes such a comment and without taking a breath ask if mornings or afternoons are best for him? As mentioned earlier this question works perfectly as it creates a diversion.

The prospect's immediate thought process is now concerned with what day and time is open in their daytimer. You have assumed the appointment or sale through the power of positive thinking and followed through to the completion of the call by securing an exact date and time. Now you will secure a firm commitment.

Do you now see the analogy between sales and theatre? Sure, the prospect only provided a one person audience, and although your performance could only be heard, the prospect was deeply moved by it. After all, you made the prospect laugh and got the prospect to participate, didn't you? Most important, though, is the fact that the prospect will remember your name and the name of your company.

Stay light, be in good spirits, put on your actor's face, and perfect your performance through daily practice. It really is a rewarding experience.

Now let us consider a phone offering that was produced and delivered by an expert that was directly involved in the training of sales personnel. The expert was making a call on behalf of the same training company.

Good morning Mr./Mrs. ………… My name is ………….. I'm with a company called Dynamo International - the sales training company.

Have you got a minute or two?

Dynamo International is a successful sales training group. During the past few years we have helped numerous companies to achieve substantial sales volume increases. We teach individual sales skills where needed and set a 3 and 6 month objectives that will enable your company to reach sales targets. We also work with sales managers in order to enhance their position and free them up to do what they do best - manage the sales force.

If you are interested in achieving immediate sales gains, perhaps we should set an appointment, at which time we can explain the benefits that our company can offer as well as, the types of contracts that are available.

Stop reading now and make a list once again of the glaring errors that were apparent during the course of this particular phone presentation. There were some positives that shone through this presentation as well. They should be duly noted as we will elaborate on them as well.

When you reread this script again, remember that we only want to get an appointment at this stage. That is the only concern.

Now let's compare notes once again.

Mistakes or Flaws

Aside from making the same basic errors as were outlined in the first sample script such as asking for a minute or two in a manner that invited a negative response and mentioning the word "appointment", what else was wrong about this presentation?

The presentation was too verbose. The salesperson was trying to cover too many points on the phone.

The salesperson in this case, didn't know the status of the sales management situation, and yet, volunteered unsolicited information that he/she works with sales managers.

Perhaps, this company was running without a sales manager and was in fact, presently seeking an individual to fill that position.

The caller in this case, failed to involve the prospect in the conversation. The salesperson did not encourage participation or dramatize even one statement in order to get some kind of emotional response. It was a very bland, non-assertive performance. By using words such as perhaps and making statements such as "what do you think?", the salesperson was indicating a lack of confidence and was inviting a negative response. To add insult to injury, the pitch ended with the mention of the word contract, a definite no-no.

The Positives

The caller in this case, without question, knew the product inside-out. The salesperson was an expert in the sales training field, and sounded very authoritative by stressing the fact that individual sales skills were taught and that certain objectives were set for a specific time period.

This information is great stuff, however, it should be used only for a back-up or fact script - and even then, with extreme caution. The execution of the fact script is to be used only when you are asked specific questions.

The proper preparation and use of the fact scripts are detailed at the end of this chapter.

Remember one thing! Never, under any circumstances, get involved in a lot of detail on the phone. Always, just get a commitment for a meeting. Meetings are the proper venue for the discussion of details.

No matter how close you are to the business, avoid detailed discussions on the phone at all times, or you are doomed to failure.

Following are some additional examples of scripts that were custom-designed for a variety of clients in the industrial and financial sector.

Brevity, regardless of your knowledge, your intellect or your expertise, is the key to success when developing your business via the telephone.

Every conceivable product or service can successfully be launched through proper use of the telephone.

Sample Sales Script #3: A Computer Education Company

Good morning Mr./Mrs. ………… My name is …...……. I'm with Correct Computer Training Co. - the micro computer educational company.

I'll just take a minute of your time. Is that alright?

The Correct Computer Company offers a specialized, educational software training program that maximizes individual performance levels through direction and support.

I have just one question to ask you:

If we could help your company personnel to achieve substantial productivity increases and greater profitability could we have 15 minutes of your time?

Are mornings or afternoons best for you?

MAKE THE APPOINTMENT

Another effective script for the same educational company would be as follows:

The Correct Computer Co. offers a specialized software educational program that maximizes individual performance levels through direction and support. We offer personalized instruction on current major applications in the micro computer industry.

The question of the day is:

If we could help your company to achieve dramatic productivity increases, could we have 15 minutes of your time?

Are mornings or afternoons best for you?

...MAKE THE APPOINTMENT

Let's look at a script that contains too much information and is too time consuming. Read the following script several times, then go back to the previous two scripts and read them.

If you were the prospect, which one would impress you?

This third script for the Computer company was written by an experienced outside representative who was endeavouring to generate more business through cold calling on the phone.

I'm with a company called The Correct Computer Training Co. You don't know me, so I'll just take a minute of your time.

Is that okay?

Correct Computer is a well known, highly regarded company in the micro computer, educational services field. We offer personalized instruction on current major applications in the micro computer industry such as Lotus 1,2,3, introduction to MS DOS, WordPerfect etc.

Our coaching programs are effective, as we limit all classes to six people at one time. These programs are aimed at the entry level position, to the most advanced applications. All packages are custom designed to best serve your company's needs.

I have only one question to ask you:

If we could precisely demonstrate, how we could assist your personnel towards becoming more productive, could we have 15 minutes of your time?

The major flaw in this script, besides being too lengthy, is that it once again, gives too much information. The more information prospects have, the more likely they are to make a snap decision on the phone. Prospects will prejudge your service and chances are that the judgement will be negative.

During the past few years, an increasing number of women and men have become the victims of attrition due to recessional pressures, ever increasing competition and automation. An unprecedented number of these people have chosen to pursue careers as consultants in their chosen fields of endeavour.

As a consultant, you are competing in major cities with dozens of other people who are offering the same services.

As an individual who is trying to launch a new business or career and develop a customer base, the phone offers great potential as your primary communicator. Phone contact can prove to be your major source for generating ideas and developing a customer base. While other forms of marketing communications do indeed deliver opportunity, none offers the combination of control factor, timeliness and benefit of personal liaison as phone communications.

Sample Sales Script #4: A Financial Service

The following is a very successful script promoting the services of a financial consultant. It was primarily used for contact with presidents of small to medium sized businesses.

Good Morning Mr./Mrs.   M y name is   I'm with First Financial Consultants. You don't know me so I'll be brief! Is that okay?

Our associate, John Doe, has impeccable credentials as a senior level banker in international banking circles. If you are even remotely considering loan negotiations with company bankers, restructuring debt, or are contemplating entry into the international market place, then John Doe merits your time.

Just one question:

If we could prove our worth to you, would it be fair to ask for just 15 minutes of your time? Are mornings or afternoons best for you?

Sample Sales Script #5: An Insurance Company

Good   Mr./Mrs. ………… My name is ………… I'm with ……………… the income replacement people here in …………... I'll just take up a moment of your time! Is that alright?

Our company is now launching a new low cost program that will protect your family against illness or accident.

I have just one question to ask you:

If I could show you how to protect your family against financial distress, at an affordable price, could I have 15 minutes of your time? Are mornings or afternoons best for you? '

Sample Sales Script #6: Accounting

Accounting (a)

Good   Mr./Mrs. ………… My name is ………… I'm with Ace Consultants - The accounting specialists.

I'll be brief!. Is that okay?

Ace Consultants is a leading accounting firm that is totally dedicated to independent business. We specialize in the areas of job project costing, property management and retail inventory.

Just one question:

If I could demonstrate exactly how our ongoing support and direction will dramatically enhance your profit picture, could we get together   ?

(WAIT FOR THE RESPONSE), THEN ASK:

Are mornings or afternoons best for you?

...MAKE THE APPOINTMENT

Accounting (b)

Good Mr./Mrs. …………. My name is …………... I'm with Ace Consultants - The accounting specialists.

I'll be brief! Is that okay?

Ace Consultants offers outstanding expertise in management, finance and guidance in government assistance and training programs.

Just one question:

If we could offer you a total solution accounting program, could we get together for 15 minutes? (WAIT FOR THE RESPONSE), THEN ASK:

Are mornings or afternoons best for you?

...MAKE THE APPOINTMENT

Accounting (c)

Good Mr./Mrs. …………. My name is ………… I'm with Ace Consultants - The accounting specialists. I'll be brief! Is that okay?

Ace Consultants offers unparalleled expertise in the areas of corporate partnership or individual taxation issues.

One question:

If we could secure meaningful federal tax rebates on behalf of your firm, could we sit down for 15 minutes?

(WAIT FOR THE RESPONSE), THEN ASK:

Are mornings or afternoons best for you?

...MAKE THE APPOINTMENT

Accounting (d)

Good Mr./Mrs. ………. My name is ………… I'm with Ace Consultants - The accounting specialists.

I'll be brief! Is that okay?

We specialize in offering fully integrated, balanced accounting systems that lead to bottom line profitability.

One thought:

If we could offer you a total solution for all your record-keeping functions, could we arrange a brief meeting?

(WAIT FOR THE RESPONSE), THEN ASK:

Are mornings or afternoons best for you?

...MAKE THE APPOINTMENT

Accounting (e)

Good Mr./Mrs. …………. My name is …………. I'm with Ace Consultants - The accounting specialists.

I'll be brief! Is that okay?

Ace Consultants is an established, well-respected accounting firm that specializes in business plans, bank presentations and integrated systems implementation.

I have an idea:

If we could give you a decided edge in your business decision-making and offer the key to future growth, could we ……?

(WAIT FOR THE RESPONSE), THEN ASK:

Are mornings or afternoons best for you?

...MAKE THE APPOINTMENT

Sample Sales Script #7: Personnel Placement Agency

Scenario: This agency has expanded its services in the areas of pay equity, salary surveys and management placement. It wants to expand its customer base and has targeted larger corporations to achieve this goal.

Good , Mr./Mrs. ………………I'm with ……………. The personnel placement people. I'll be very brief! Is that okay?

Our company has now expanded our services to address areas of concern that are facing most businesses in today's marketplace.

The only question that I have is:

If we could prove our worth to you in the areas of pay equity, salary surveys and management placement, could we have 15 minutes of your time?

Are mornings or afternoons best for you?

Sample Sales Script #8: An Automobile / Car Dealership

Good morning Mr./Mrs. …………… I'm with …………… your local …………… dealer. I'll just take 30 seconds of your time. Is that okay?

Our company has just developed an innovative low cost leasing program that makes our X, cars more affordable than ever before.

If you are even remotely considering a new automobile in the near future, we would like to get together with you for 15 minutes. Is that a fair request?

Are mornings or afternoons best for you?

Sample Sales Script #9: A Real Estate Company

Good morning Mr./Mrs. …………… This is …………… I'm with …………… here in town. I'll keep the conversation very brief! Is that okay?

Our company has developed an enviable referral program, locally, due to our outstanding service and integrity.

If you are even remotely interested in listing your home at the highest possible market price, we would like to have a confidential meeting with you. Is that a fair request?

Are morning or afternoons better for you?

Sample Sales Script #10: A Newspaper

Good   Mr./Mrs. ………… My name is ………… I'm with the Senior Citizen Review –

The authoritative Seniors paper in …………

or

- The leading Seniors' paper in …………

I'll be brief! Is that okay?

Our paper specializes in reaching the affluent over 50's segment of our population.

One suggestion:

If we could offer you an advertising vehicle that will dramatically increase your sales, could we have 15 minutes of your time?

(WAIT FOR THE RESPONSE), THEN ASK:

Are mornings or afternoons best for you?

...MAKE THE APPOINTMENT or an alternative close

If we could demonstrate precisely how The Senior Citizen review could help your company to meet or exceed specific revenue targets, could we get together for 15 minutes?

Other Alternative Closes

1.   If we could offer an affordable alternative approach to reaching affluent prospects could we discuss our strategy for success with you?

2.   If we could maximize the results of your advertising budget dollar. could we...?

3.   If we could offer a refreshing new approach towards increasing sales and profits could we...?

4.   If we could optimize your sales through a creative new approach to advertising, could we...?

5.   If we could target your advertising to reach those consumers with the greatest disposable income in Canada, could we...?

6.   If we could offer a concrete advertising strategy that will significantly increase sales, could we...?

Note:

Any of the aforementioned questions can be converted into an assertive statement which could be used in your opening. For example, we specialize in maximizing the results of your advertising dollars (refer to alternative #3). Your closing statement in the form of a question (called the hook) could then be selected from one of the other closing statements that best matches this specific opening statement. Example #6 would fit here.

Sample Sales Script #11: A Water Treatment Company

Water Treatment Company (a)

Good .... Mr./Mrs. .... M y name is .... I'm with Clear Water Industries - The Water Treatment Specialists.

I'll be brief! Is that okay?

Clear Water offers quality, full service water treatment programs for virtually every application in the industrial sector.

Just one question:

If we could demonstrate exactly how we substantially reduce maintenance costs, could we get together for a few minutes?

or alternative opening

Clear Water offers leading-edge technology in the water treatment field in virtually every industry that employs water in it's daily operations

Water Treatment Company (b)

Good .... Mr./Mrs. .... My name is .... I'm with Clear Water Industries - the Water Treatment Specialists - the Industrial Corrosion Specialists

I'll be brief! Is that okay?

Clear Water offers quality, full service water treatment programs to virtually any industry that employs water in its daily operations. We provide quality - engineered solutions for industrial corrosion, process cooling and heating and waste water applications.

One last suggestion:

If we could substantially, reduce maintenance costs and maximize profits, could we have 10 minutes of your time?

Other Alternative Closes

1.   If we could offer you an affordable alternative to equipment replacement costs could we have 10 minutes of your time?

2.   If we could dramatically increase the life of your system (equipment) and substantially reduce equipment expenditures, could we have 10 minutes of your time?

3.   If we could show you exactly how our management program will increase employee productivity, could we have 10 minutes of your time?

4.   If we could substantially reduce maintenance costs through a customized monitoring program, could we have 10 minutes of your time?

5.   If we could dramatically reduce your downtime and increase you uptime, could we have 10 minutes of your time?

6.   If we could demonstrate cost-effective solutions to any and all water-related problems, could we have 10 minutes of your time?

7   If we could offer you better service, faster reaction time at a reduced rate, could we get together for a few minutes?

Sample Sales Script #12: A Furniture Store

Sample Script (a)

Good .... Mr./Mrs. .... My name is .... I'm with Perfect Furniture Ltd. - the Modular Office Specialists

I'll be brief! Is that okay?

Perfect is a highly successful office systems manufacturer that specializes in maximizing productivity levels. We accomplish this through ergonomic design and innovation.

Just one question:

If we could demonstrate precisely how our unique design concept dramatically reduces facilities management costs, could we get together for 15 minutes?

(Wait for the response!)

Are mornings or afternoons better for you?

MAKE THE APPOINTMENT

Alternative Closings Using The Hook

1.   If we could show you the most cost-effective office planning and management system ever devised, could we have 15 minutes of your time?

2.   If we could demonstrate a remarkable modular office furniture system that is in total harmony with today's computerized environment, could we have 15 minutes of your time?

Sample Script (b):

I'm with Perfect Manufacturing - A world leader in modular office furniture systems. I'll be brief! Is that alright?

Perfect markets the only ergonomic modular desk system in North America. It is regarded as the most user-friendly system ever developed and offers a perfect fit for today's computerized office environment.

If we could offer you an environment that will dramatically increase productivity levels AND greatly enhance company morale, could we have 15 minutes of your time?

Alternative Closings

1.   If we could introduce you to a system that will result in a more effective, focused and motivated work force, could we have 15 minutes of your time?

2.   If we could offer you a custom designed system that addresses all ergonomic concerns AND that will meet or exceed all management expectations, could we have 15 minutes of your time?

3.   If we could offer a system that minimizes downtime during installation AND maximizes uptime upon completion, could we have 15 minutes of your time?'``

Sample Script (c)

Use the opening as shown in script (a) or (b). Use the following for the main body of your offering.

We provide leading-edge approaches to the development of a flexible and cost-effective office and workstation environment.

Just one question:

If we could show you exactly how our ergonomic desk based system totally eliminates maintenance/installation personnel, thereby reducing costs, could we have 15 minutes of your time?

Alternative Closing

If we could offer a refreshing new approach to office furniture design that is end-user driven, could we have 15 minutes of your time?

Sample Script (d)

After opening, insert the following:

Precision offers a menu of approaches to the development of modular office furniture systems to suit any budget.

Just one question:

If we could offer you an ergonomics-based system that would maximize your systems budget dollar, could we have 15 minutes of your time?

Alternative Closing

If we could show you a cost-effective modular system that will substantially reduce employee fatigue AND optimize productivity levels, could we have 15 minutes of your time?

Sample Sales Script #13: A Propane Reseller to Consumer or Industry

Good …………… Mr./Mrs. ………… My name is ………… I'm with Propane Unlimited - the Motor Fuel Specialists.

I'll be brief! Is that okay?

Propane Unlimited offers an affordable alternative to conventional gasoline. Our product - liquid propane gas - is clean, plentiful and inexpensive.

Just one question:

If we could offer you a safe, efficient motor fuel that will dramatically reduce your fleet operating costs, could we get together for a few minutes?'

(Wait for the response)

Are mornings or afternoons best for you?

MAKE THE APPOINTMENT

Additional closing statements, in question form, that could be used in order to evoke a positive response are as follows:

1.	If we could demonstrate exactly how propane could reduce your downtime and increase your uptime, could we have 15 minutes of your time?

2.	If we could offer you an affordable solution to rising fleet operating costs, could we get together with you?'

3.	If we could offer you a cost efficient program that will dramatically reduce your fleet operating costs AND increase profitability, could we talk?

4.	If we could dramatically increase efficiency levels AND reduce costs, could we have a few minutes of your time?

5.   If we could offer concrete ideas that will substantially increase productivity levels, could we have a few minutes of your time?

6.   If we could demonstrate that propane dramatically reduces engine maintenance costs, could we have a few minutes of your time?

7.   If we could offer you substantial savings in fuel costs, could we have a few minutes of your time?

Note:

Any of the aforementioned questions could be converted into an assertive statement that could be used in your opening. For example, We specialize in reducing operating costs by offering a safe, efficient motor fuel alternative. Your closing statement in the form of a question (called the hook) could then be selected from one of the other closing statements that best matches this specific opening statement. Example #7 would fit in this case.

By constantly interchanging your opening and closing statements, you will keep the script fresh and will be assured of maximum impact. Dozens of combinations are possible using this method.

It is equally important to insert the prospect's name throughout the script. By personalizing your scripts, you are making a statement that you really do care about the prospect and their business. Specific examples of how to personalize scripts are detailed in Chapter IV.

All of the scripts that you have read, although designed for entirely different industries have several things in common. Pause, for a moment if you will, and list them on a note pad.

If you mentioned brevity you already have one correct answer. If you mentioned the fact that all scripts strictly highlighted the service or product involved you are on your way to becoming a sales superstar. The other common traits that these scripts possess include a sense of urgency, a sincere promise of results, and an overwhelming desire to be of service.

Now that you have learned how to write a script, the next logical step is to learn how to read or act out the script in an effective manner.

Acting Out Your Script

Now that you have developed the perfect script, it is almost time to put the idea to the test. But first you must learn to present your idea in a natural manner that does not sound like you are reading from a textbook. Proper script layout will assist you with this effort.

One method that works extremely well is to leave an open space in your script when you come to the key or power words that you want to emphasize. These words should be in bold faced type. You could also use a highlighter on them for your own emphasis and reminder. When typing your statement always be sure to use double or triple spacing between lines. You will then be able to make additions or deletions as you gain experience. More important, you will be able to read the script in a more effective manner.

As a specific example of how to space or group words in accordance with their importance, let's refer back to the first script that concentrated on selling lift trucks. Pause with each gap in the script for added emphasis and impact.

Good morning Mr./Mrs. ………… My name is ………… I'm with a company called ABC Canada

<   > The materials handling company.

You don't know me so I'll be brief< > Is that okay?

ABC Canada < > SPECIALIZES < > in improving the COST EFFICIENCY < > and

< > FLEXIBILITY of materials handling requirements. We have experience in a wide variety of industries < >.

I have only one question to ask you. < > If we could SIGNIFICANTLY < > LOWER your handling costs < > and < > DRAMATICALLY increase you PROFITABILITY <> could we have 15 minutes of your time?

Reading Rehearsals

Before refining your voice in addressing the intricacies such as inflection, intonation, rhythm and other advanced theories, practice at just being yourself

Put a smile on your face and speak directly into the mouthpiece. Your smile will help your voice to take on a pitch that is pleasant to the listener's ear. Read relatively slowly and place emphasis on those key words. Practice reading newspaper advertisements out loud after you have read them over to yourself several times:

You could even use a highlighter to emphasize those words that you think are most important to the success of the advertisement. Don't be concerned if at first, you stutter and stammer slightly or insert a few "uhs" in your script. Despite these flaws, your presentation will sound better than if the listener can detect you are reading a pitch word for word from a script.

Listen carefully to radio and television announcers and learn how they use their voices to their best possible advantage.

Developing a Secondary Fact Script

It would be so easy if all your prospects responded in a positive manner at the conclusion of every presentation. Although many prospects do in fact, say "yes" immediately and agree to a meeting without hesitation, many will first want to have a few questions answered.

It is for this purpose that we develop the fact script. It should be readily available to you at all times and should be typed out in point form only. Once again brevity is very critical here. Answer one or two questions at most, and then proceed to the close again.

If the prospect persists with detailed questioning, assure him or her that the sales rep will respond to any and all questions at the time of the get together. Be polite, but firm. Suggest that a face to face meeting is always best.

Anticipated questions should be listed in advance on a back up script sheet with the answers listed in point form. This format should apply to all salespeople regardless of their experience.

Always remember, the salespeople who give the most detailed answers over the phone, are the ones who secure the fewest number of face to face appointments. They have given so much information that prospects feel that they can make an educated purchase decision. Nine times out of ten, the decision will be a no.

Let's examine four examples of secondary fact scripts:

Sales Training Company

Some common questions that might be asked if you are selling this type of service are: What do you do?

How do you go about doing that?

At this stage, without skipping a beat, you refer to your fact script and make two or three of the following points:

- We customize our training program to suit your company's needs.

- We coach and develop your people.

- We teach sales skills where needed.

- We build an active sales plan.

In most cases, the above information is sufficient to close the appointment. If not, you will have to switch over instantly to a new tactic which is outlined in the Overcoming Objections section.

The important thing to do right now is to develop a secondary fact script that succinctly outlines your company's service in a brief as manner as possible.

Always remember, that the longer the conversation continues, the less likely your chances become in securing the appointment. Hit two or three highlights of your product or service and try for the close immediately. Be brief, be courteous and stand firm that you will answer any and all questions at the time of your meeting.

Newspaper

A secondary fact script for a Seniors Newspaper publication would reinforce your primary target market. The following facts could be noted:

                            John Peaker

- Seniors market growing - in 12 years the over 50's population has jumped by 26% to X million people.

- The over 50's population control 80% of wealth.

- The Senior Citizen Review has proven to provide the most effective delivery of the advertising message to this affluent market.

- Mention distribution numbers i.e.: 20,000, 50,000, 100,000.

- Mention new distribution channels such as retirement homes, clinics, hospitals, libraries etc.

Other Benefits

- 13 point type face - easy reading.

- 99.5% pick up every issue published.

- Local flavor - profiles on local - senior personalities and comprehensive local content.

- The most read senior community newspaper.

- A retention rate of up to two (2) months compared to one day retention rates of the dailies.

- A high impact publication that gets results at a fraction of the cost associated with the major dailies.

Propane

If you are selling a relatively new product or an alternative fuel product such as propane, it is inevitable that you will be asked questions. Be prepared.

Following are some samples questions on the use of propane and some suggested, concise responses that you could offer.

What is Propane?

Propane is a liquified petroleum gas, commonly referred to as LPG. Propane is the fuel with higher octane and increased combustion efficiency.

What about performance?

Propane powered vehicles are noted for fast starting and smooth, knock-free flow when pulling away or passing other vehicles.

What about availability?

Propane is readily available right across the country and is not subject to foreign embargos or shortages.

What do propane powered vehicles look like?

There is no visible difference until you look under the hood or under the vehicle itself where the tank is located.

If you have mentioned reduced engine maintenance costs and are asked to explain, be prepared with a straightforward statement such as:

Propane powered vehicles consistently enjoy extended engine oil and spark plug life, and should experience much longer intervals between engine tune-ups.

Immediately following your response to the question, use a second or even third close to get a positive response. Try to match your close with that of the last question. Based on the aforementioned question, you might want to close the appointment with the following:

If we could demonstrate exactly how propane dramatically reduces engine maintenance costs, could we have just 15 minutes of your time?

(Wait for the response)

MAKE THE APPOINTMENT

Water Treatment

Some key points that might be applicable to this type of service are:

- Clear Water has been in business since ....

- One-stop water treatment company. We have laboratory facilities for analysis purposes and in-house research facilities plus expertise in production development.

- Our microbiological program utilizes two main products and a third product that offers a back-up solution.

- We address scale control and corrosion control.

- Offers corrosion protection for all ferrous and non-ferrous metals.

- Use unique water use monitor equipment.

In summing up this section on the development of secondary fact scripts, remember the following four rules:

1. Be prepared

2. Be brief

3. Be reassuring

4. Be in the closing mode after each statement

IV.   HOW TO DEVELOP EFFECTIVE PHONE TECHNIQUES

A good actor must portray a specific role in a poignant manner in order to create credibility with the audience. You must also learn to project your own personality to your audience or prospect in a manner that states emphatically that you are believable. You must be able to convince your audience that the product or service that you are selling can offer immediate benefits.

The word "tele", contained in the word telephone is derived from a Greek term meaning at a distance. Selling from a distance is far more difficult and complex than selling someone who is sitting across a desk from you. The prospect is not influenced by your dress, your physical appearance, your smile, your gestures or any other personal mannerisms.

The only asset that you have at your disposal is your voice. You are, in fact, acting out a telephone commercial for your product or service. To become a top telephone actor requires that you develop the voice of a radio announcer, the stamina of a long distance runner, and the selling skills of a professional salesperson. Perhaps above all else, you must have a burning desire to succeed and the heart and courage to make that next call after experiencing rejection on the previous one.

Following are specific attributes and skills that must be acquired and developed if you aspire to be successful in telephone communications.

Actor's Phone Techniques

As a telephone actor - who is acting on behalf of your Company - you are playing the role of an interpretive artist rather than an original artist. You are conveying the company's words, ideas and feelings to the audience. Working within the company's concept, it is your responsibility to interpret the presentation's meaning and to transmit the presentation's emotion to the audience.

As you are giving a solo performance, it is up to you, and you alone, to recognize and evaluate the prospect's response to whatever is said during the presentation. Being in such a unique position requires that you be prepared - after your performance - to either correct or enhance the response that is being conveyed by the prospect.

It is this ability, either innate, acquired or both, that separates the elite communicators from the mediocre. Unlike the theatre actor who must remain within the strict guidelines of the script, the telephone actor has the flexibility to dramatically change the presentation to suit the personality type of the one-person audience.

A phone sales performance is similar to performing on the high wire at a circus. One thoughtless comment, one omission of detail or even one clumsily worded statement could spell disaster.

It is, therefore, critical to rehearse your presentation, including the overcoming of objections, prior to going on the air. Your responses must become automated and delivered in an articulate manner if you are to achieve that emotional impact that is necessary for success.

The Actor's Responsibility

The phone actor's (salesperson's) primary responsibility is really very straight forward. First, as a representative of the company, you are expected to portray a whole picture of the company image in as few words as possible. A poorly portrayed presentation can destroy the relationship between the actor and the audience.

The Actor's Medium

As a phone actor, you are working with limited resources, and have only yourself to build upon. You are both artist and medium. It is your mind, experience, imagination, and capacity to feel and understand that enables you to conceive the character that you will exhibit to your audience - the prospect.

It is with your words that you make your concept audible and comprehensible. The voice alone is capable of conjuring up an image in the mind's eye of the audience of something that is either highly desirable or unimportant. In order to create an image of desirability, the actor must learn to employ the voice in a manner that can reflect compassion, surprise, delight and a sense of urgency.

Let's take a close look at the mechanics of how the voice works and how it can be projected for maximum results.

Voice Projection Techniques

As air is expelled from the lungs, it passes through the trachea or windpipe through the lips of the larynx. These lips are known as vocal cords. When the vocal cords are pursed or tightened, the air passing between them causes them to vibrate and produce sound. By varying the tautness of the cords, the speaker is able to vary the pitch of the sound.

The sounds can be strengthened by increased pressure from the lungs and is amplified by certain cavities or bone structures in the head, throat and chest known as resonators. Some resonators such as the nose and sinuses do not change in shape or size. Others such as the mouth and larynx are adjustable and can be changed in size and shape. These are the ones that form the vowel sounds.

The sounds produced by the vocal cords, formed and amplified by the resonators must be further shaped into consonants, syllables, and words to produce intelligible speech. This function is performed by the tongue and lips and is known as articulation or intelligible speech.

Sound is produced by taking air into the lungs and expelling it through the tightened lips of the larynx, causing the vocal cords to vibrate and produce a sound. The more pressure there is behind the expelled air, the louder will be the sound.

The sound is enriched and amplified by resonators and by the mouth and the lips, then released in the form of syllables and words. Good speech with standard pronunciation and well-articulated syllables and words will set you apart from your competition.

Poor or sloppy speech with badly articulated words, pronunciations and faulty inflections will be instantly detected. The audience will be aggravated by unpleasant sounds and will be distracted from considering your offering if they have to decipher your words.

It is important to concentrate on words that you are having difficulty with or to replace them with synonyms (words that mean the same thing). Always keep in mind that simple words are the most effective words. If you are unsure of proper pronunciation, consult a pronouncing dictionary of American English (Merriam-English) for final determination.

Goals of Good Speech

If you are to achieve the desired emotional response from your audience, they must be able to hear you. Many phone communicators maintain their volume levels during the first few words of a sentence, only to trail off towards the end of the sentence. Unfortunately, as the final few words are usually the most important, the overall impact of the point being made is substantially reduced because the final few words uttered seem to lack true conviction.

Although projection of the voice is normally associated with increased volume, it is a generally overlooked fact that proper projection is directly linked with proper breathing procedures. Improved breathing techniques can be achieved through the correct use of the diaphragm in order that the lungs will always contain enough air to support the sound, and sustain it to the last syllable of the phrase or sentence.

One exercise that you might practice to improve breathing techniques is to inhale deeply, tighten your stomach muscles, and read a short sentence as you slowly exhale. Repeat the exercise with each sentence, read and gradually increase the length of the sentences read. Proper breathing will become second nature with constant practice.

Many salespeople, although they have mastered correct breathing techniques and are capable of maintaining adequate volume levels, are afraid that they will appear to be shouting at their audience.

Always remember, it is better to be too loud rather than too quiet. Volume levels can always be adjusted downwards as you gain experience. Although maintaining volume levels is important, other attributes such as the articulation of consonants, contribute to the overall effectiveness of voice projection. Words and syllables that sound clear, distinct and well separated, rather than jumbled, leave a lasting impression with any audience.

In order to achieve improved articulation try keeping your jaw completely relaxed and your mouth opened wide. Most important, slow down your presentation and concentrate on being more articulate.

You may be conscious of a slower pace, however, your audience will fail to notice any discernible difference and will, in all probability, be more appreciative of what you have to say.

To Be Intelligible
Although they understand what they themselves are saying, many sales people leave their audiences wondering what has been said. Somehow the meaning of the presentation itself, although close to achieving its goals, leaves the audience unclear as to what the real objective is all about.

For this reason, it is critical that you practice your presentation on someone far removed from the business who can remain objective. By doing so, you can test your intelligibility and make the necessary adjustments to the content of your script or presentation.

The art of being intelligible or understood depends on the clarity of your offering. In order to achieve superior clarity in your presentation, close attention must be paid to enunciation of each syllable and word to ensure that words are not slurred.

Inflection refers to the change of pitch in your voice, either upward or downward in order to achieve emphasis or to add a dramatic tone to your presentation. Inflection could also indicate a complete change of direction in your thought process and most certainly should be used in the hook at the conclusion of the presentation when you are endeavouring to illicit a positive response by asking a question.

Although it is virtually impossible to speak a single sentence without using inflection, the secret to using inflection effectively is to learn exactly when to employ an upward or downward variation of pitch. By changing the inflection from one word to another, you will be better able to achieve emphasis while holding your audience's attention.

Assume that you are endeavouring to secure an appointment with a prospect and would like to reinforce your sincerity, as well as show respect for your prospect's valuable time. You might want to make the following statement:

I **guarantee** that we won't waste your time. It will be time **well** spent. The words in bold type face should be emphasized through voice inflection. Timely pauses also serve to highlight the critical use of inflection. One of the most effective pauses that an experienced salesperson learns to employ is illustrated as follows:

I have just one question to ask you! The pause after that statement sets the stage for what could be the **close** of the appointment or sale. It is a dramatic pause that indicates the importance of what the sales person is about to say next. The manner in which inflection is used reflects importance.

Intonation

Intonation or colouring as it is sometimes called, combines the change of pitch and the increase or decrease in volume with a variation in the tempo or rhythm. It's purpose is to give words or phrases a greater meaning and to illicit an emotional response from the audience. One such example of intonation would be as follows:

If we could show you **exactly**, how to **increase** your uptime, and **lower** your downtime, could we have just 15 minutes of your time? The words in bold type face are spoken slowly and deliberately. There is barely a discernible pause just prior to or after uttering these key words. Let's take a close look at the mechanics of this skill.

If we could show you (slight pause) EXACTLY (slight pause) how to INCREASE (slight pause) your UPTIME (slight pause) and LOWER (slight pause) your DOWNTIME, (slight pause) could we have just 15 minutes of your time?

The reading tempo is increased significantly, both before and after the key words in the statement.

Practice this one statement until you feel comfortable with it. The next step is to act out the statement with someone who hasn't heard it before and get their honest assessment of how it would be received by a complete stranger.

Sales people who achieve a dynamic clarity of offering reflecting precise enunciation, timely use of inflection or pitch, proper execution of the pause, and intonation for that extra dramatic effect, will have a tremendous edge over their competitors who don't know how to use these skills.

If you want to rise above the crowd, you must constantly practice these voice and presentation skills on a daily basis. You may feel uncomfortable at first using these techniques, however, with time, patience and constant rehearsal, they will become second nature to you.

Developing a Pleasant Voice

It is obvious, to most people, that in order to succeed in the selling profession, one must develop a voice that is vocally pleasing to the ear. Although very few of us are blessed with a radio announcer's voice, we can, through proper exercise, find a voice level that is acceptable. A voice that is either too high or too low, is not an interesting voice, but rather is considered to be a monotonous voice. In order to find the ideal range of your voice, which, for most people is the middle register, try the following exercise:

Close your mouth and start to hum. Through self discovery, you will find that you can direct different notes to different resonators in your throat and head. You will know when you have located the right resonators by the intense vibrations that you will feel in that area. Through ongoing practice, you will be able to automatically direct the right tones to the correct resonators. This will improve the overall resonance of your voice.

The most important characteristic that a salesperson's voice can possess is variety. Variety can only be achieved through the acquiring of flexibility in your use of volume, inflection, voice colouring and emotional intensity.

You must learn to breathe deeply and to control the release of breath with skill and technical expertise. It is essential that you be able to let the voice out, or hold it in, and still be heard clearly by your audience:

Once your voice is trained and possesses true variety, you will have developed a sales tool that will prove to be an invaluable asset in dealing with people at any level.

You will be heard, you will be believed, and you will be remembered!

Developing Assertiveness

The verb, assert, means to state positively or to affirm. Synonyms for the word assertiveness, a noun, include the following: positive, decided, dogmatic, and aggressive.

A person who lacks assertiveness or the ability to become assertive, should not be involved in the sales profession.

The prospect on the other end of the phone can easily ascertain whether or not you are confident in yourself and in the product or service you are selling. If you allow even the slightest trace of tentativeness to creep into the conversation, you are done like dinner.

Think positively at all times. Be assertive to the point of being aggressive and you will succeed. Always remember that you are the one with the hammer and that you are expected to be on the offensive - not the defensive.

Selling is like a war. As in warfare, you launch an all- out offensive with every weapon in your arsenal. You hold back nothing or you will achieve just that - nothing.

One of the most glaring examples of a non-aggressive statement usually occurs at the very beginning of a presentation when the salesperson is asking for the decision maker. Many salespeople start out by asking if Mr. Smith would be available. The question is worded in such a manner that it is almost an apologetic statement and does not express a sense of urgency, or a real strong desire to speak to Mr. Smith.

Mr. Smith's secretary will sense your tentativeness and dismiss your call as a waste of Mr. Smith's time. She will in all probability, politely state that Mr. Smith is in a meeting and is not available.

The opening question indicates right away that the salesperson is already in trouble. In all probability, this type of person is also very likely to ask the prospect when it would be convenient for the prospect to see them. By so doing they are opening the door to rejection rather than acceptance.

In sharp contrast, the assertive salesperson's opening statement is direct and positive. Mr Smith please, indicates to the secretary that this salesperson is serious and business-like. It also implies that the salesperson knows Mr. Smith (although in all probability he does not). Mr. Smith's secretary is very likely, in this case, to ask who is calling and put the call through without delay.

Do you see the difference between being assertive as opposed to non-assertive? It's the subtle differences that separate the top producers from the also-rans.

In our first example, the non-assertive salesperson asked when it would be convenient for the prospect to see them. What do you think the answer would have been?

In nine calls out of ten the answer would have been negative. The real professional, the assertive salesperson offers a choice by asking: if mornings or afternoons are best. The prospect's mind shifts gears and concentrates solely on whether a morning or afternoon is best and on what day this assertive salesperson could best be accommodated.

If the prospect had any doubts as to whether he or she would see the salesperson, they have completely been dissipated as a result of the pre-occupation with setting up a meeting. This assertive salesperson assumed the sale, or in this case, the appointment, by thinking positively and envisioning success.

Simple, isn't it? This technique really does work, if you set your mind to achieving success on every call, and, follow the methods illustrated. Once you have made hundreds of calls, your sense of timing will become so precise that the results will amaze you. So start making those calls right NOW! Maintain your assertiveness on each and every call, and your cold call success will skyrocket.

Effective Use of The Pause

Most salespeople are so obsessed with securing the appointment, or getting the order, that they are almost hyper-ventilating. If you are one these people, slow down your RPM's and learn how to use the pause to your advantage.

The pause can be used effectively for the following purposes:

- To build a relationship

- Highlight your company's services

- Emphasize key words or power words

- Develop trust

- Close the sale or appointment

Each of the above objectives can be achieved through the subtle use of the pause. The time duration factor for each pause will vary, and will depend to a large extent on, when, where, how and for what purpose it is to be used.

Pausing To Develop A Relationship

If a salesperson asks how you are and it is asked in a sincere manner, it would be common courtesy to wait for a response. Wouldn't you agree with this statement?

Believe it or not, the vast majority of salespeople do not wait for an answer, but rather start right into their pitch. The total disregard for the prospect's feelings is, quite frankly, like a slap in the face. Take the time to pause and wait for a response, if you hope to build any kind of relationship. If you have acquired a bad habit of not pausing after you have posed a question, it is possible to curb the habit by writing in the word Pause after the last word of the question and highlighting it with fluorescent Highlighter.

Pausing To Highlight Your Company's Services

Once you have stated that you represent a specific company, you should pause for a brief second or two, and in three or four words, tell exactly what it is that you do.

Example:

I'm with Tele Dynamics International <Pause> The Business Development People!

The pause is effective in that it very briefly tells the prospect the nature of your business up front. It piques the interest and immediately sets the stage for the main body of your script.

Aside from using the pause, you should deliberately use the word "the" when describing the business on whose behalf you are calling at the time. Do you understand why you should employ such a simple three letter word as "the"? The word the, although simplistic in nature, carries a lot of weight. It implies that the company on whose behalf you are making the pitch, is recognized as being 'the authority' on the subject matter that you will be describing with this particular prospect.

*Please note that by using the word "the", you are not misleading the prospect in any way, but rather are using the word to emphasize that you are proud of your product or service and are competent at that which you do. If you did not feel strongly about your company, you should probably not be in the business.

Pausing To Emphasize Key Words or Power Words

When using the pause to emphasize a key word, the actual length of the pause is really just a fraction of a second, and yet it can mean the difference between success and failure. Although the length of the pause in terms of time, seems like an eternity when you are reading your script, it (the pause) is not even discernible to your audience. The reason for this is that the word you have just emphasized flashes in the prospect's mind like a neon sign.

Practice reading this statement over and over again until you feel that your timing with The Pause is precise.

If we could show you <pause> exactly <pause> how we could raise your profits, <pause> and <pause> lower your costs, could we have 15 minutes of your time?

NO two people will read this statement in exactly the same manner; however, those that read it effectively, will have acquired the skill to combine precise timing with a versatile voice that reflects unceasing and unbridled enthusiasm.

Pausing To Develop Trust

For illustration purposes, consider a hypothetical situation whereby a prospect is almost on the verge of agreeing to an appointment. They still have some doubts however, as to whether or not they should give up valuable time to see you. After all, they don't know you and have never heard of your company. One method of gaining trust is to make the following statement:

I **guarantee** <pause> that we won't waste your time. It will be time <pause> **profitably** spent!

When one has been candid, so sincere and so considerate of another person's time, it is awfully difficult for a prospect to turn around and say no. Wouldn't you agree?

Pausing To Close The Sale Or Appointment

If there is one pause that <u>must</u> be mastered, this is the one. It is the most difficult type of pause for salespeople to adjust to as it can involve a lengthy waiting period in dead silence.

After the closing statement, in the form of a question that has been delivered, the prospect is supposed to say "yes" immediately. In the real world, this is not always the case. As a matter of fact, very often the silence on the other end of the phone is so pronounced that you feel as if you have butterflies in your stomach and your brain has become paralysed.

Ten seconds pass, then twenty, or more and you feel as if you have waited ten or twenty minutes. Still no response, still DEAD SILENCE! What do you do now? Do you break the silence and try another close? Do you continue to wring your hands and wait some more? How do you handle this unbearable pressure cooker?

The answer is that you WAIT - YOU WAIT or you LOSE! It's as simple as that. Remember that the prospect is under the gun, so to speak, just like you. You have thrown the ball into the prospect's court. It is the prospect's turn to respond, not yours. The salespeople who can exhibit self-discipline have the odds heavily stacked in their favour. In order to help you cope with this unnerving situation, here are some tips that work extremely well. You will probably develop some of your own methods in dealing with what is really psychological warfare.

During the pause, slowly write the word "yes" or "sold" beside the name on your lead sheet. Another idea that eases the pressure is to peruse your day-timer for open days and possible appointment times. On some occasions, you might actually work out your commission on the sale and transfer it to your daily tally sheet.

Any personal gimmicks that you develop during the pause, reflect your vision of success. Every thought is positive as you refuse to let negativity even enter your thought process. By thinking only positive thoughts, you can transfer positive thoughts to your audience - the prospect. It will work for you.

Personalizing Your Scripts

Do you like to hear your name mentioned when someone is talking to YOU? Of course you do! It is the highest compliment that one individual can pay another individual. By inserting a specific name throughout a script, you are really saying: "I care". Your presentation leaves the impression with your prospect, that you have custom designed your presentation solely for that individual.

It conveys the impression that the prospect, at that specific moment in time, is the most important person in your life. In conveying the importance of your prospect's well being, you must truly believe in your own heart and mind, that the product or service will enhance that person's personal advancement or business development.

Personalization of a script is really a self-taught skill that requires constant practice and precise timing on the part of the reader or presenter. All salespeople will ultimately develop a personalization technique that is unique to their own style. The important thing to remember is that the style you use must sound natural - as opposed to contrived. It must come across to the prospect as being totally sincere in nature.

If the timing in the personalization of your script does not feel comfortable in your own mind, chances are very good that the prospect will not feel comfortable either.

It is possible to effectively personalize your script by using several different approaches. Assume that you are calling customers or potential customers to whom you have never spoken, to invite them to a two-day warehouse clearance sale.

The purpose of your call blitz is to attract as many potential clients as possible to attend your special event.

After the traditional opening statement, your conversation could be personalized as follows:

> Janet, we are extending an invitation to you, as we know how important price and quality is to your business!

Another alternative is as follows:

> We are extending a personal invitation to you, Janet, as we know the importance of price and quality in today's business environment.

A third alternative to the individual pitch, would be as follows:

> We a extending a personal invitation to you, as we know, exactly, how important price and quality are to you, Janet.

During a complete presentation, you should insert the person's name at the beginning, as well during the main body of the presentation, and always at that point in time when you employ The Hook to close the sale or appointment.

By personalizing your script, you most certainly will be better able to hold the attention of your audience, and sound more professional in the delivery of your message at the same time.

Return now to previous scripts and practice personalizing them. Practice until you feel completely confident that you will be able to employ this skill in an effective manner, without interrupting the flow of your presentation.

Maintaining Continuity and Effectiveness in Phone Communications

A common problem associated with inside sales is the risk of early burn out. This malady can be avoided if you take the time to develop into a real professional, with versatile scripts and outstanding delivery techniques.

One method that works well is the development of a minimum of three or four scripts for each client or product line. Although the purpose of each script is to deliver the same message, by rewording certain key points, you will be able to maintain a fresh outlook day-in and day-out. Your first priority is to secure as many appointments early in the day, through the utilization of a script with which you feel most comfortable.

You could then change over to other scripts and challenge yourself to deliver them in an as effective manner as the one with which you are most at ease. By alternating scripts, you are also constantly changing the various elements and emphasis that goes into the delivery of the most successful pitch.

Each script tests your acting ability to the utmost as you are forced into changing intonation, personalization order, and timing, to best suit the specific script that you are using at the time.

If you are able to adapt to any number of different approaches, you will find immense satisfaction in your efforts. You will feel refreshed, and most importantly, your audience - the prospect, will welcome your approach if it translates into a dedicated breath of fresh air to the ear. The secret is to make each performance sound like your best performance of the day. It is a formidable but rewarding task.

Another effective method that can be used in order to avoid the burn out problem, is to physically stay active throughout each day in order to keep the circulation levels up, and the blood pressure levels down. If you are working in an office that has stairs, use them rather than taking the elevator. Stand up every so often, and practice touching your toes, or do some stretching exercises by using your desk as a stationary support.

Extend your arms against the edge of the desk or heavy chair and stretch the muscles in your legs as you lean forward. Alternate each leg for maximum benefit. Walk to lunch and back rather than taking the car. Practice making a few calls from a standing, rather than a sitting position. It may take some time before you are comfortable with this one, but rest assured that it will become second nature after a while.

Psyching Yourself to New Levels of Achievement

Psyching is a word that is derived from the verb "psych", meaning to make mentally ready, as by inducing alertness or tension.

The psyching we are referring to here, is the ability to stay up for every call. It is the mark of only a relatively few salespeople who make it to the top of their profession.

Psyching, as it relates to the communications aspect of the selling profession, is directly related to the ability of the salesperson to express emotion in an uninhibited manner.

You can personally psych yourself up by building on success. After you have made a call that has resulted in a sale or appointment, applaud yourself in the form of a gesture such as a handclap or a shout, or both! Exercise your emotions, and let your victory be known to yourself.

Although others may hear your vociferous antics, it only serves to spur them on to meeting or surpassing your successes.

You are not making noise to draw attention to yourself, but rather to create enthusiasm within yourself that cannot, and will not, be extinguished. It allows you to build up your momentum and confidence to such a high level that you will feel like a tidal wave about to swallow-up the shoreline or anything else that gets in it's way.

Psyching enables you to feel good about yourself and your achievements. It really doesn't matter what others think about you. You are accountable to yourself in the selling profession, and in the real world, your success or failure rests solely on your shoulders. You must learn to use and reuse any device that works to your advantage.

Practice Sessions

Theory is helpful, script writing essential, but practice is reality.

You will find that it is a great practice to use role playing in honing your phone skills. If there are several salespeople involved in phone sales, the leader should designate one person to play the role of the prospect, one to be the salesperson and the third person to act as an observer. Have the salesperson make the call to an extension phone with a speaker.

In this way, the observer will be able to listen to the conversation and offer a constructive critique on the call. Roles are interchanged until everyone has had the opportunity to become a salesperson, prospect and observer. It is important to always stress the positive aspects of each person's call in order to build the other's confidence.

Of course, it is important to offer suggestions on how the call or certain aspects of it could be improved, but please be careful not to embarrass or mock the salesperson who has made an obvious gaff. Treat one another as you yourself would like to be treated.

Several different exercises can be handled in a like manner. For example, the leader could stress that all first calls are to be concerned with content. The second round of calls would be concerned with voice projection. The third call could be an exercise in assertiveness, while the fourth call could be dedicated to the overcoming of objections.

The final step, would be practice on the complete call, including the close. The possibilities for further practice sessions are only limited by your imagination.

The important thing to stress during these practice sessions is that they are intended to provide constructive criticism only, and that you want the participants to have fun while learning. If the sessions are handled with discretion, enthusiasm will abound, and you will be on your way to developing a cohesive, well-prepared sales team.

Group training should not stop with just one or two sessions, but rather should be conducted on a weekly basis. The salespeople should keep updated notes on details of specific areas where they experienced objections or difficulties that they were unable to overcome. These problem areas should then be addressed at the weekly group meetings before they are forgotten. No matter how trite a specific problem may appear, it should be solved before it becomes a larger roadblock to the individual's success as a salesperson

V.   OPENING NIGHT: THE FIRST CALL

The curtain goes up and you're on the air with your first live commercial. Doesn't it feel good to get those first jitters out of the way? Congratulations! Some of you may have just taken that first small step that will lead to giant steps in the enhancement of your sales career. It was not easy, but you broke the ice. Now you can concentrate on becoming a force to be reckoned with in the future.

It is important that you do not put too much pressure on yourself during those first few days. They should be used primarily to become comfortable with the scripts and in talking to your prospects. Relax and have a little fun. When you do speak to someone, speak to them as you would your best friend. Use your phone at work as you would use it at home.

It is not uncommon for a new salesperson to run into a string of rejections during those first few days. Don't become discouraged or dejected. Treat rejection as just another stepping stone to success, and, above all else, do not take rejection personally. During these first few days on the phone it is wise to record all objections that you encountered and had difficulty in handling.

Also, be aware of the various responses you received. Be totally honest with yourself and you will able to improve your weak areas and build on your strengths. Let's examine how you can become a more effective communicator by developing a vision of success.

Envisioning Success

Always remember that if you think that each call made will result in an appointment or a sale, your chance of success will dramatically improve. The secret to being successful on the phone is to treat each phone call or contact, as you would a personal face to face meeting. You must envision yourself shaking hands with the prospect, introducing yourself and your company, and being invited into the prospect's office for a confidential meeting.

Although you are unable to see the prospect, or make physical contact, you must be able to transfer your mental energy into the thought process of the prospect. Unlike a personal face to face meeting, when you, perhaps, might be able to warm up the prospect through trite conversation, you cannot afford this luxury on the phone.

You must instead, come across immediately, as a warm, caring, individual, with a genuine interest in the prospect. It is a lot to ask of a person given a time frame of between five to ten seconds, isn't it? It is, however, possible to achieve this objective through the tone of your voice, your inflection and superb timing.

These three skills, tone, inflection and timing, take the place of that trite conversation that occurs in a face to face meeting. You can imagine what would most likely happen if, for example, you started talking about the weather on the phone. You would be talking to yourself after about ten seconds had elapsed.

If you have managed to win the acceptance of the prospect to the point where the prospect is at least willing to listen to your presentation, you have a 50/50 chance of success. The ratio of success will now rise or fall on the balance of your presentation. The ball is in your court. If you have come this far and have won the acceptance of the prospect to continue, your confidence level should be on the rise.

As your confidence level has increased, your main statement should reflect that confidence. As you deliver your statement you must always envision success at its conclusion. That vision of success will, no doubt, be reflected in your voice, and will be transferred like a bolt of electricity into the mind of the prospect. By envisioning success throughout the entire statement you will be subconsciously setting the stage for a favorable response from the prospect.

Assuming that you have now progressed through the entire statement without interruption, you now have the prospect 90% sold. However, like the saying: Close only counts in horseshoes, you still have to take that final step and clear the last remaining hurdle - if your call is to be deemed successful. That last hurdle is the close.

It is at this stage in the presentation - when your confidence level reaches a new high – the hook is delivered with such conviction, that the prospect can feel your positive vibrations on the line. Those vibes should be so powerful that the prospect cannot possibly reject the proposal of such an optimistic and dynamic personality as yourself.

It is also important to envision that the next presentation will be delivered with even more zeal and dedication than the previous one. Aim to achieve higher and higher degrees of excellence, day-in and day-out, and you will achieve an amazing success rate on your cold calls.

Making the Right Impression

Everyone, at one time or another has received a phone call from someone who is trying to sell something. Think back for a moment and try to remember a salesperson whose presentation on the phone actually resulted in an appointment or your purchasing a specific product or service. Now try to remember exactly what attributes that the particular salesperson exhibited that sold you on their product or service. Note the information on a piece of paper.

Let's list a number of positive traits that a good salesperson might exhibit in order to make the right impression.

Caring	Enthusiastic
Pleasant	Brief
Authoritative	Confident
Sense of Urgency	Low key

Humble   Sincere

Forthright   Polite

Once you are able to incorporate all of the above characteristics into a professional presentation, and are able to deliver that presentation in the smooth manner of a seasoned radio announcer, you will indeed have made the right impression. Rehearse it, nurse it and rehearse some more.

Once you have made a number of calls and have listed any problems that have arisen, review this next section on the evaluation of your performance. The questions that are asked should be answered in an objective manner as they will provide an invaluable insight into your problem areas or weaknesses.

Although your presentation may seem to be virtually perfect, you might be able to detect just one small flaw that is preventing you from becoming far more effective and successful.

It is a good idea to purchase a tape recorder in order that you will be able to do a proper analysis of your techniques. Just as the top golf professionals review their swings on video tape with their professional instructors, so should you constantly review your verbal selling techniques.

Evaluating Your Performance: Avoiding the Pitfalls
Following is a list and review of some of the most important questions to ask yourself when you begin the evaluation process.

Speaking with Authority:

How often are you able to reach the decision maker?

If your answer is seldom or fairly often, the indication is that you are being almost apologetic or lacking aggressiveness at the reception or secretarial level.

A statement asking if Mr. Smith would be available for a minute, indicates an apologetic approach and a lack of confidence. Try changing your approach to reflect a more positive and authoritative stance. "Mr. Smith, please!" sounds much more business-like and indicates a sense of urgency and authority. You are assuming that you will be transferred to Mr. Smith without delay. It works!

Volume Levels:

Listen carefully to your voice for volume levels. Do you keep your voice loud enough to be clearly heard at all times? In a thirty second commercial, every word spoken is important. It is therefore very critical that your prospect hears and understands every single word in your presentation.

A very common habit that many salespeople develop is to let their voice trail off towards the end of a sentence. If anything, volume levels at the end of the sentence should be rising, not falling. It is your intent to build suspense, to create excitement, to entertain, and to act out your script in a manner that will hold your audience's attention right up to the climax. Strive to consciously maintain adequate voice volume levels throughout the entire script and you will achieve the desired effect.

Reflecting Enthusiasm

Listen carefully to the taped version of your presentation. Does your voice reflect immense enthusiasm over the product or service you are offering? Unless it does, your chances of success are greatly diminished. How in the world do you expect a prospect to get excited, if you're not excited? You must convey the message that you can hardly wait to make a personal, face to face presentation to the prospect. That enthusiastic energy will then be transferred into the mind set of your prospects, to the extent that they will actually be looking forward to meeting you.

The next time you make a particularly enthusiastic phone presentation, listen carefully for the response. There is a very good chance that the prospect will state that he is looking forward to meeting you: I look forward to meeting you. If you are able to consistently solicit this type of response from your prospective clients, it goes without saying that by exhibiting immense enthusiasm, you are an enthusiastic person.

People like to talk and meet other people who are enthusiastic. Maintain your enthusiasm, build on enthusiasm and sell enthusiasm. It can be your greatest strength.

Developing Assertiveness

Are you coming across to the listener as being assertive, or do you sound tentative or unsure?

You are the person who, after all, has initiated the call, and it is therefore assumed that you are the authority on the subject matter. The very instant that you may hesitate or waffle on a simple question is the instant that your credibility goes out the window. When a crack appears in your credibility you might as well forget it. There is no going back.

Although you may have a good handle on your business, it is the manner in which you respond to an unexpected question that is the guideline by which a prospect measures your credibility. Equally important in the prospect's mind, is the time frame in which you answer the question.

A response to any question must be almost instantaneous in order to project that assertive and authoritative image. The response should be honest, and should be delivered with sincere conviction. It should leave no doubt in the prospect's mind that you know exactly what you are talking about.

One example in handling an unexpected question with expertise and assertiveness is as follows:

Scenario:
You are calling a prospect in a specialized industry about which you know very little. Your client database indicates that you have never dealt with any company in that particular industry.

The prospect asks if you ever done work with any company in his industry? What would your response be to this question? Think about it for minute!

The reply that you might employ for an instant response is that you have not; however; your service is transferable to any industry.

This response is honest, it indicates adaptability, and, spoken with conviction asserts that your company is confident that you can do the job, and achieve the desired results without any difficulty.

Always remember, you are the authority in your field. Deliver each statement in an assertive style that reflects that authority. It will erase any and all doubts that may exist in the prospect's mind.

Following A Script

Do you follow a script to the letter and place emphasis on key words, or do you ad lib and interpret the script as you proceed? If you want to make the proper impression, and have an impact on the prospect, it is imperative that you sound like a professional.

Following a planned script is the only sane approach to take in the development of sound phone marketing practices. As previously mentioned, you must discipline yourself to become comfortable with the sample scripts that were provided earlier.

Constant practice will ensure your comfort with any script. A properly read script will leave a lasting impression on your prospect. Just as professional radio or television announcers carefully rehearse their scripts, so should you rehearse your presentation. Even if you have read a script a hundred times, it is critical that you rehearse that same script before you start your calls every day.

The pre-call warm ups will help you to exercise your voice and develop a rhythm that will put you in midday form in the early morning hours. You should constantly experiment with new delivery methods in order to improve your rhythm, timing, and overall effectiveness. No matter how adept you may think you have become, there is always room for improvement.

Using the Hook to Your Advantage

Are you using the hook and, if so, are you using it effectively?

The reason the hook was designed in the first place, was to make a strong statement to the prospect. The statement made in the guise of a question, virtually guarantees a yes response. The prospect is really placed in a position between a rock and a hard place. To say no makes the prospect feel foolish.

The only logical response is to say, "yes". The hook, when used skillfully, with proper emphasis on key words, is probably the most important tool that you have available. Use it on every call to your full advantage.

Building On the Successful Call

Do you tend to become discouraged after two or three consecutive rejections?

Sales prospecting by phone, at times, will prove to be very demanding on your patience and on your mind. It is psychologically very demanding and extremely difficult to stay up for every call. The inside sales call function requires a special ability to set your mind on automatic pilot and to ride through the storm clouds until you hit sunshine once again. Experience will teach you to never take a break from your phone routine after you have received two or three consecutive rejections.

Quitting, even for a few minutes, on a down note, makes it all the more difficult to get back into high gear. Therefore you must discipline yourself to persist through these rejections until you get a winner. Once you are back in the winner's circle, deliberately speed up your dialling pattern in an effort to close two or three more prospects.

You can then take a short break to rest on your laurels and replenish your energy. Your confidence levels will be high as you resume your calling responsibilities. It is much easier to build on success than it is to try to rebuild on failure. If you adhere to this philosophy, each and every day will be successful. It will work for you!

In the evaluation of your performance, there are numerous other factors that can make the difference between success and failure. Some of the other questions that you should ask yourself, are listed below. Your forthright answers will obviously help you to overcome your weak areas and turn those weak spots into strengths.

Do you fold at the first objection, or do you fail to handle objections to the listener's satisfaction?

The one category that stands out as being the most important aspect in the entire sales process, is the overcoming of objections. Overcoming objections is truly an art that must be nurtured and developed over a period of time. This art form must be mastered if you hope to be successful in professional selling.

Objections on the part of a prospect, cannot be put on the back-burner, to be dealt with at a later date. They must be dealt with instantaneously. The response to any objection should be honest, credible, and wherever applicable, should be backed up by facts. Salespeople must be able to overcome objections by providing a logical, straightforward rebuttal to the objection in a diplomatic manner.

If you are experiencing difficulty in the overcoming of objections, you will want to read the next chapter entitled How to Overcome Objections.

Do you listen to what the prospect has to say to you?

It is absolutely astonishing just what you can learn about a prospect and the prospect's business in a relatively short period of time. Most salespeople people fail to capitalize on information that is being offered to them, because they have developed a form of tunnel vision. They have their own focus, with one simple objective - to ram the product that they are selling down the customer's throat.

These salespeople lose out because they have failed to hear the prospect's cries for help. Their self-inflicted deafness does not enable them to do some investigative work on discovering or uncovering the prospect's hidden needs.

The following is an actual documented case example of a materials handling salesperson who took the time to listen.

The salesperson contacted a major corporation on behalf of a leading materials handling company. The logistics manager informed him that he had recently purchased several used pieces of equipment and that spending on capital equipment had been frozen indefinitely. He pointed out that a presentation would be a waste of time. The salesperson agreed with him completely.

Fortunately, the salesperson had the foresight to ask the prospect what type of equipment he used and how many units were employed in his warehouse operation. As a direct result of the salesperson's investigative questioning, he secured an appointment for his company's service manager to meet with the prospect.

The end result was that the service manager sold a two year preventive maintenance contract to the company worth thousands of dollars. Developing good listening habits pays big dividends.

Turning Negative Statements Into Positives

When a prospect is completely negative to your presentation do you also become negative and give up?

Next time a prospect makes one negative statement after another, take the following approach:

- Let the prospect get rid of all frustrations. Don't interrupt, but rather wait until the prospect is completely finished.

- Sympathize profusely with the prospect's situation or past experiences. In as few words as possible, repeat the problems back to the prospect.

- Now that the prospect knows that you have listened to all the specific problems, a tenuous allegiance of sorts has been formed. The next step is to offer your help in the most sincere manner possible.

- Restate the benefits that your company can offer and name a referral company in the same industry that benefited from your service. Don't be afraid to state what sets your company apart from your competition.

- Ask for an appointment in a very low key manner and emphasize that it will be a no-pressure, non-committal meeting. Assure the prospect that the meeting can be terminated after the first five minutes if the prospect does not like what you have to say.

In many instances where negative comments are made by a prospect, it is simply a case of the prospect being short changed in the past. The old adage once bitten, twice shy, certainly applies to hundreds of companies who have paid for services, but did not receive good value for the money spent. It takes a very caring and skilled salesperson to overcome the objections of any prospect that has been victimized.

Maintaining a Proactive Rather Than a Reactive Stance

Are you being proactive or reactive? Do you maintain an offensive position about the benefits that your company offers, or, do you let the prospect control the conversation and dominate you?

Many prospects, by nature, enjoy dominating a sales call because they can disrupt the flow of a script to the point where the salesperson becomes lost, and ultimately surrenders. You need not be victimized by this kind of prospect. The secret in handling this type of individual is to keep your cool and to create a mental book mark at the exact point in your script where you were interrupted.

Once the prospect has completed off-the-cuff' remarks, you simply continue the presentation from the point where you were so rudely interrupted. The prospect will then respect the fact that you are the authority, and will, in most instances, retreat from an antagonistic position. You will then be able to use the hook to reel-them-in.

Stay focused, stay mentally alert, maintain an unwavering confidence level, and you will win your fair share of these extremely trying calls.

Asking For The Appointment

Do you ask for the appointment once, receive a no, and then just hang up?

If this is the case, then you are really missing the boat. Statistics indicate that at least 15% of prospects say no at least once, before they say yes. Can you imagine how much your income level would rise if you could learn to convert the no's into yes's? Several conversion methods can deliver amazing results. The first, and most straight forward method to apply after receiving the one word response NO, is to counter with a one word response of your own.

Simply ask, "Why"?

This one word "why", completely throws the prospect off the track. The prospect really doesn't know what to say to such a direct one word question. Quite often this method will break the prospect up into laughter. This pause for a little humor will open the door for you to repeat the benefits and go for a second close. It takes guts to pull this one off, but it is amazingly successful.

The use of one simple word, "why", sounds so juvenile, doesn't it? - and yet it is so very, very powerful! Next time you get a no to the closing question, respond by immediately asking, Why? You'll have some real fun with this one.

Another effective conversion method, is the humorous approach. Immediately after receiving a no from the prospect, make the following statement!

You're the very first person that has ever turned me down.

Then deliberately pause and wait for a response. It is the prospect's turn to speak so wait for that response. Almost without exception, you will receive a roar of laughter on the other end of the line. The tension has been broken, and the door reopened to the renewal of your presentation. Just carry on as if the word "no", had never been mentioned and try again for the close.

Laughter or humor, as it relates to the selling profession, plays an indeterminate role in overcoming seemingly huge obstacles or objections. Loosen-up and laugh with your prospects, for laughter indeed, works wonders.

The third method that you might consider in your rebuttal to a no, is the one which employs the pleading approach. This approach sounds something like the following.

> Please don't say no - at least not yet. You could be depriving your company of renewed profits!

This reply to a "no" response, is so unique that it too evokes laughter and comments from the prospect.

It buys time for a continuance of the conversation and enables one to slip in another one or two benefits, without appearing to be overbearing or high pressure. You then ask for a commitment.

Using Brevity to Your Advantage

Do you find yourself being drawn into a long-winded conversation with certain prospects?

One of the major common pitfalls that must be avoided at all costs, is the giving out of too much information. The more information that you give out over the phone, the more inclined prospects are to make negative decisions. Prospects that are trying to spare themselves the time and aggravation of granting you an appointment - unless you can justify it to them on the phone - are doing both parties a grave injustice.

It is virtually impossible for the prospect to obtain enough detailed information on the phone about your service, in order to make a rational decision. Similarly, your inability to gain an accurate analysis of the prospect's needs leaves you in an extremely disadvantaged position.

To be certain, you cannot avoid the prospect's questions altogether. That would result in disaster. You should however, answer several questions in as brief a manner as possible using your secondary script.' After you have answered two or three questions, you should make the following statement:

> I have an idea. Let's get together for 15 minutes, at which time I will answer any and all questions that you might have concerning our service!

Then immediately follow up with another hook by asking if the request for 15 minutes sounds reasonable. Most prospects, will then agree to see you. If there is still some hesitation after you have used the hook, insert the following statement:

> We won't waste your time. It will be well spent.

If you have answered all the questions in this evaluation process with complete honesty and objectivity, you will have been able to pinpoint your weak areas. It is now up to you to turn these weaknesses into strengths by reviewing what we have covered thus far and practicing your techniques through on-the-job training.

Nothing can take the place of those contacts with real prospects in the very real world. As we continue to read and work our way through the subsequent chapters, you will find the answers to any and all problems that you will encounter.

Be patient, follow directions and always envision success.

How To Get Past The Receptionist Or Secretary

In smaller companies, many salespeople find themselves being confronted by receptionists who take it upon themselves to ask pointed questions about the nature of the phone call. Many salespeople state the general nature of their business and are immediately informed by the receptionist that the company doesn't need that service. These salespeople accept this information, hang up the phone, and go on to the next call.

It doesn't have to be this way at all. The receptionist, in most cases, has obviously been told by the boss to screen all calls and is simply following orders. Unfortunately, some receptionists carry their screening orders to extremes, as they are totally intimidated by their superiors. They are determined that if the person's name and company are not known to them, the call will not be forwarded, period.

So what do we do to get through that iron curtain screen in order to reach the decision maker?

The approach that you might find to be most effective is the no-nonsense approach. Say good morning, or good afternoon, to the receptionist and repeat the receptionist's name, if in fact, it was used in the initial greeting.

Ask directly for a specific person, (if the name is available to you) and WAIT.

When confronted with a decision-maker style receptionist who might ask what is this call in regards to? You could reply in your most sincere voice, that rings with a sense of urgency...

My call is a confidential business call.

Confidential is a very intimate word with many connotations. In nine calls out of ten, your call will be put through to the decision-maker.

Always give your name, and the company you represent to the receptionist. If requested to spell your name, do so. Pronounce the name of the company you represent clearly and slowly, no matter how small or insignificant it may be, as though your company is a well known Fortune 500 firm.

In larger companies where the management people have personal secretaries, you will have to pass another screen test - getting by the secretary to the decision maker. No problem!

Most secretaries mention their name and the specific name of their department. Since you already have the name of the person to whom you wish to speak and the name of the secretary, politely greet Effie and ask for Charlie in an affirmative manner.

You have been courteous, direct, and completely business-like. By using Effie's name and Charlie's name it sounds very much like you have spoken to Charlie Clinker before, doesn't it? Should the secretary also ask about the reason for your call, stay with your original game plan and state that your call is of a confidential nature.

The No-Names Receptionist

In some instances, you may not have the name or names of any company personnel. You call and are told by the receptionist that she is not allowed to give out any names, period. If the company is a large corporation, you could ask for the personnel department. Generally speaking, personnel people are very understanding and will direct you to the correct party. If personnel won't give out any names, they will transfer your call to the secretary of the department head that you are trying to reach.

When the secretary answers the phone, listen very carefully, as the response will normally indicate the person's office that you have reached. Without blinking an eyelid you then ask for that person by name. If the party is not available, you at least have the contact name to ask for in your follow-up call. Most important, you will avoid any confrontation with the company receptionist on subsequent calls and your call will be put through immediately.

In dealing with smaller companies you could ask for the shipping department or the order desk. When someone picks up the phone, proceed with a condensed version of your sales pitch. In most cases, the party to whom you are speaking will interrupt with the terse comment that you have contacted the wrong department At this point in time, apologize profusely and state that obviously the receptionist had you transferred to the wrong extension. You then ask for the correct contact person.

In most cases, the person involved will give you a name. Ask for the correct spelling of the individual's name. If the name is difficult to pronounce, print it out phonetically in block letters. This practice will pay dividends later when you actually speak to the prospect.

Another alternative approach in solving the problem of reaching the decision-maker is to call between 8:00 am and 8:30 am before the switchboard opens and between 5:00 and 5:30 after the switchboard closes. You may have to start earlier in the morning and finish later at night, but the results will astound you. The boss never works 9-5 and you will have a direct line to the decision maker.

Always remember, if you have the will, you will discover innovative ways to circumvent the uncooperative receptionist or secretary. Your very livelihood may depend on it. All it takes is a little imagination on your behalf and a whole lot of sheer persistence and determination.

VI.   HOW TO OVERCOME OBJECTIONS

We have now arrived at the most critical part of the book, and the most important aspect of the entire sales process.

We will be spending an inordinate amount of time on this section in order to cover a full range of objections that you will be facing in the real world. Today's business climate is like a battlefield that is filled with land mines. They have to be avoided if you are to survive. The prerequisites to survival are courage, faith and the ability to listen, think quickly and react decisively under pressure.

There is a commonality to any and all objections that are encountered. Whether you are selling tangibles or intangibles, it really doesn't matter.

The thing to remember is that any objection, large or small must be handled expeditiously and confidently if you are to succeed.

Assume that you own a sales training company that specializes in helping companies to increase their sales volume levels.

You have made your phone presentation, have asked The Question, in the form of a hook and are waiting for a response. Let's look at a number of common negative responses or objections and how the salesperson managed to overcome them.

Objection #1

Prospect: No.

You: That's the first time anyone has ever said "no" to me. (prospect laughs)
                Seriously, please don't say no - not yet! You may be overlooking a very valuable
                source of profit. One question:

Prospect: Go ahead.

You: Are you willing to consider new opportunities for increased profitability?

Prospect: Of course. That's a stupid question.

You: We are the best in our field and can provide references.

Prospect: Okay. But don't waste my time.

You: I guarantee that it will be time well spent.

Prospect: Okay! But you've only got 15 minutes.

Objection #2

Prospect: I get 5 mailings a week from companies like yours.

You: Do you know where you should file them?

Prospect: Where?

You: In the trash! (prospect laughs)
Seriously, we've been in the business 6 years and offer customized programs that address specific needs.

Prospect: Who have you done business with in my industry or neighborhood?

You: We just finished working with ___. and they are elated with the value received.

Prospect: Oh.

You: Are mornings or afternoons better for you?

Prospect: Early AM is the best. Let me check my calendar.

Objection #3

Prospect: We don't need anyone in here telling us how to sell. I do the training myself.

You: You handle all the training?

Prospect: That's right! I've been in this business for 25 years, you know.

You: Sounds like you must be doing something right. You are obviously very successful.

Prospect: Yes we are!

You: You know I have an idea! Perhaps we can further enhance your program. We all learn something new every day. Right? (Prospect agrees)

Prospect: I suppose it wouldn't hurt to talk to you, but I won't commit myself.

You:	It's a strictly non-committal meeting. Are mornings or afternoons best for you?
Prospect:	How about Thursday at 3:30?

Objection #4

Prospect:	Send me some literature and I'll look it over and call you back.
You:	I'd be happy to send you an overview, however I think you can appreciate that everyone's needs are different.
Prospect:	I know that, but I still need some information about who you are before I'll see you, and I would also appreciate some references.
You:	No problem. I'll tell you what I can do right now! I'll send you all the information via e-mail today. All I ask is that we schedule a meeting for next Tuesday or Wednesday. Is that fair?
Prospect:	Oh alright! But call ahead the day before to confirm.
You:	Thank you. I'm confident that our meeting will be of great benefit to you.

Objection #5

Prospect:	No thanks. We just signed up with Mister Toastmaster for a six month program.
You:	Well that sounds great! I took that course and found it to be very beneficial.
Prospect:	Really! You know we believe in training courses and send all our people on them at least once a year.
You:	Good idea. You know Ms. Prospect that our function is completely different than the Toastmaster program.
Prospect:	How's that?
You:	They teach public speaking skills and how to conduct oneself in front of groups. We are different in that we actually coach your people on individual selling skills.
Prospect:	I'm willing to listen to any idea that will improve my sales.

Objection #6

Prospect: It's my month end. I can't make any appointments right now. I'm going crazy!

You: I can understand your situation. Isn't it amazing how quickly time passes? I hadn't realized that we are almost at the end of ………..

Prospect: You're right ... and then next month, it's our year end.

You: Since we both have to work around busy schedules, let's tentatively set up a meeting for next Tuesday at 2:00 PM.

Prospect: I'm really booked for the next two months and I'll be out of the country after that.

You: You're a busy person. I don't mind meeting very early in the morning or late in the afternoon. What time do you start in the morning?

Prospect: 8:00 O'clock.

You: How would it be if we meet at 8:00 AM next Monday? That way the balance of your day will be free.

Prospect: Fair enough. See you then.

Objection #7

Prospect: Our sales are fine!

You: Do you have a system in place for measuring individual results? Is each salesperson hitting their monthly targets?

Prospect: Well, not really. We're almost even with last year. That's not too bad considering the economy. Our sales people don't really have targets. If they don't sell they lose out on commission.

You: If we could show you how we can increase your sales volume by 5% or better, would you talk to us?

Prospect: Just exactly how do you plan on doing that? I doubt you can do it.

| You: | Well, for one thing we formulate a sales plan that concentrates on sales activity for 30, 60, or even 90 days. I am very confident that you will be impressed with our program. Nothing ventured, nothing gained. Right? |

Prospect: I'm at least willing to listen to anyone that can increase sales.

You: You won't be disappointed. How's next Wednesday?

Objection #8

Prospect: That's one of the best sales pitches that I have ever heard, but I still don't know what you do.

You: We conduct a complete discovery of your objectives and make recommendations that will achieve the desired results.

Prospect: Give me more details about the rest of the program and it's contents.

You: I am more than willing to do that Mr. - - -, however a face to face meeting is always best as everyone's needs are different. I'm sure you're aware of that, aren't you?

Prospect: I'm not really sure if you could help us.

You: To be honest, I'm not sure if we have a fit or not. Mr. - - - -. I can tell you, however, that we have a 98% success rate and the references to back that up. I'm sure that we'll both be better able to make an accurate assessment within the first 10 minutes of our meeting.

Prospect: You certainly are persistent. Alright. I'll try to squeeze you in next Monday. How much time will it really take?

You: To be honest, 30 minutes should be more than adequate. Thank you very much.

Objection #9

Prospect: I haven't got the time, I fired two of my four sales people, including the sales manager and now I'm on the road part time myself.

You: That being the case perhaps we can help you out of your predicament.

Prospect: What do you mean?

You: One of our key functions is to act as a part time sales manager for small to medium sized companies. It is a role that we have successfully played many times in the past.

Prospect: Could we meet at 7:30 - 8:00 AM? It's the only time I really have to myself.

You: The earlier the better. I love to get a head start on the day.

Objection #10

Prospect: How much money is this going to cost?

You: I really can't answer that question Ms. ______ until we determine exactly what your needs may be. Our company policy allows us to work within any spending guidelines – large or small

Prospect: The boss has to approve any purchases and she's not too keen on spending money.

You: Might I suggest that all three of us get together. Let's set up a tentative date right now! What day looks good for you next week?

Prospect: I'll set aside 30 minutes for you to make a presentation this Friday.

You: Thank you. We'll look forward to seeing you next Friday at 8:30 AM.

Objection #11

Prospect: Thanks anyway. We have in-house training.

You: Just one question: Is your training on product knowledge?

Prospect: Yes. We have a very technical product that is sold through the ability of the salespeople to explain its various functions. If they can do that the product sells itself.

You: Our company teaches actual selling skills from entry level through top advanced sales techniques.

Prospect: I don't think it would work. As I mentioned before, the product is very technical in nature and you wouldn't be able to relate. Our salespeople are all engineers.

| You: | The skills we teach are transferable to any industry. We have dealt with a number of industries whose product line is very complex in nature. We can give you specific examples. |

| Prospect: | I'll listen to what you have to say, but it better be good. |

| You: | You won't be disappointed. It will be time well spent. |

Objection #12

| Prospect: | Your program sounds impressive, however; we're restructuring and adding to our sales force, call me back in 6 months. |

| You: | I understand your going through some complex changes. You know Mr. Prospect, maybe we can help you immediately. |

| Prospect: | How? |

| You: | Our company gets involved from the early planning stages right through to the writing of proposals. Our personality type program could help you immeasurably in your sales search. |

| Prospect: | Sounds interesting! But I want you to know up front, that I won't guarantee . anything! |

| You: | It will strictly be a non-committal meeting. How about 1:00 PM tomorrow? |

| Prospect: | See you at 1:00 PM. |

Objection #13

| Prospect: | Can you cure the economic woes facing this country? |

| You: | We're good, but not that good. (prospect laughs) |

| Prospect: | We have a sales force that is in total disarray. They are devastated by the economy and the competition. Both they and myself really don't know where were going from day to day. Unless you can straighten out this government of ours, we're in trouble. You couldn't help us. |

| You: | I know were in tough times. That's why we're so busy. Your problem is quite common, believe me. You'd be interested in knowing that we just completed an assignment with a company in your industry, and their shipping can't keep up with the orders. |

Prospect: You're joking!

You: No I'm not. We'll even give you references to back up our success stories.

Prospect: Can you see me today?

Objection #14

Prospect: Sounds impressive! However, we don't have any outside salespeople. Thanks for calling.

You: Just a quick question. If you don't have sales people, how do you sell your product?

Prospect: We have ten inside sales people. All our business is conducted over the phone.

You: Very interesting. That makes a lot of sense. You know Ms. Prospect, we have worked extensively with inside sales people. Do these sales people actively seek new markets for your product?

Prospect: They are supposed to explore new markets, but they're turning into order takers.

You: We would like to show you exactly how our program could help you. Is that a fair request to make?

Prospect: Sure. I'll give you some time.

You: Let's set up a convenient time right now.

Objection #15

Prospect: You're a week too late! We just signed up for a training seminar at the Marriot Hotel with your competition.'

You: That's great! Obviously you see the merits of ongoing training.

Prospect: We spend a lot of money on sales training as we think it is very important.

You: Do you mind telling me the name of the company that will be conducting training?

Prospect: It's the ABC Motivational Company, you've probably heard of them.

You: Yes. I have heard of them. They have an excellent reputation. You'll be interested to know that ABC is really not competing against us at all.

Prospect: Don't you do the same thing?

You: No. We're not motivators as such. We offer hands-on coaching at your place of business over a predetermined time period. We teach individual selling skills and work closely with your sales manager to enhance his position.

Prospect: Do you sell tapes?

You: No. We're not into tapes. We specialize in group sessions and have designed a unique program that ensures active participation by each and every sales person.

Prospect: I think I'll let things rest for now and see what kind of results we get. Call me in 3 - 6 months.

You: We have no intentions of supplanting your present program, however, if we could show you exactly, how we can enhance it, could we at least talk to you about it. It would strictly be a non-committal meeting.

Prospect: Sounds like a fair request. When would you like to get together?

The ability to overcome objections distinguishes the super sales achievers from the mediocre. The simple way to overcome objections is to use the following structure:

A)   Begin to comply, repeat objections

B)   Ask one or two questions

C)   Give a new benefit

D)   Close again by using a different hook that fits that benefit

A number of additional objections are not really bona fide objections but rather can be classified as excuses. Chapter IX How to Close the Sale or Appointment, succinctly outlines how to recognize these excuses as buying signals by developing sharp listening skills.

VII.   HOW TO BUILD A CUSTOMER BASE

How to Create Success Stories to Open up New Markets

Whether you are an independent business person - or part of a multi-conglomerate - it is vital that you learn to adapt your product or service to fit new market client needs if you are to create new successes in unpioneered markets. Any small success in new market development for your company, lends instant credibility with prospects.

Consider this example of how one company deviated from their traditional target market and boldly focused on penetrating a previously uncharted market.

A sales training company made the decision to offer training services to lawyers. Why lawyers you might ask. They asked the same question. Think about it for a minute! Lawyers, like any other business people must sell their services to new clientele if they are to expand their client base.

Lawyers are generally very lacking in sales skills and traditionally rely on referrals to build their business. In recessional times however, a laid back approach does not work in any business. The only alternative is to become proactive if one is to survive.

After numerous rejections, the sales training company, scaled down their elongated program and offered one-half day seminars, specifically designed for the legal profession. Shortly after the launch of this condensed program, one small legal firm was secured as a client. The client was so elated with the results, that they agreed to provide a reference.

The sales development company now lists numerous law firms as clients. The key to success was the demonstrated ability to adapt to client needs and to offer an innovative program to a profession that has severe time-constraints on employee availability for specialized training.

The single, most important tool that you have at your disposal is, and will always be, THE PHONE. You must take that one success story and ballyhoo it to everyone who will listen. You must speak with confidence and authority. To do so, will ensure success after success.

Most important, don't give up with that first or fifteenth rejection. Learn from rejection, adapt, innovate and new markets will open up for you.

Following is a basic outline to help you expand the marketing of your product:

A Proposal For The Expanded Marketing of (Our Company)

Objectives:

Strategy:

Prime Purchasers: (list 5 or 6)

Secondary Purchasers: (list 5 or 6) Distribution Base:

Coverage: Who? When? Where? The Product/Service Line:

Time Planning:

Client, Agent, Purchaser Coordination:

Sales Strategy: The exact role to be played by the sales department in providing lead generation for the launch of your new offensive.

Using Success Stories To Expand Your Geographic Market Base

Market Base

All successful, well-established businesses have one thing in common. Their account base is spread across a wide geographical area. They have employed success stories to build regional business markets.

How is this accomplished? How quickly can it be achieved? To answer these questions, let's look at how proper planning, combined with an effective telephone campaign can achieve the desired results.

The first step is to determine two or three market areas where you would like to distribute your products or market your services.

The second step is to plan your phone marketing campaign in such a manner so as to devote equal time to each specific development area. By so doing, new clients will come on board at approximately the same time period in each of the two or three market areas. Now the stage is set for real market penetration.

The third and final stage, and the most important, is how to properly use the phone to create a snowball effect that will achieve all your sales objectives.

In addition to using all the phone techniques and skills that were discussed in previous chapters, here are some additional and reinforcement techniques that can make a positive impact on prospective clients.

- When talking to a client mention the name of a specific company with whom you are doing business. Mention the first and last name of your contact. Ask the prospect if they know the company.

- Listen carefully for speech mannerisms that are peculiar to the area you are calling. Adjust your tone or speech to resemble that of the prospect.

- Imply that you do business on a regular basis in the client's area. A visit is not out of your way at all.

- Keep abreast of the local news in all areas that you are calling. Make comments, if and when appropriate, on business and/or local interest stories.

- Speak to the prospect in as neighbourly a voice as possible. After all, you do have an interest in their community. You work there, don't you?

- Avoid using pressure tactics. In smaller towns or communities the use of any semblance of pressure will only create insurmountable barriers. Many business people in smaller communities do not like to commit to exact times for meetings. They just don't want to feel obligated. If this is the case, fine, back off and suggest a specific morning or afternoon. Mention an approximate time and get approval. You may wish to send an e-mail in order to confirm the date and appropriate time of arrival.

- Another approach that is effective, is to mention how satisfied the prospect's neighbour is with your company's product or service and that you would like their (the prospect's) valued opinion as to whether your product or service might be of benefit to them in the future.

- If you are working in an outlying area and have only one or two firm commitments lined up for the day, take the shotgun approach to securing further appointments. Although this approach appears to contradict earlier mentioned rules in getting firm commitments only, it does make sense if you have spent 3 hours in travel time one way for only two appointments.

How To Use The Shotgun Phone Approach

When you encounter a high degree of reluctance after making your pitch, tell the prospect that you will be in the area on a specific day and approximate time.

Ask if you could just drop in, leave some information and spend only 5 minutes in making their acquaintance. Ask the following question:

Is that a fair request?

WAIT for a response. Most individuals are reasonable if your request for their time is reasonable in nature. Once they are assured that you won't waste their time, doors will open. Don't ever abuse this confidence.

The most important objective is to open new doors, to make the initial contact and get out as promised. Rest assured, the prospect will remember your courtesy and grant you another meeting.

In summation, the secret to expanding your geographic market base is repetitiveness. Keep making those cold phone calls on preset days, followed up by personal face-to-face meetings. Be consistent, stay focused and you will get positive results.

How To Develop A Market Niche.

The dictionary defines "niche" as any position specifically adapted to its occupant, or a recessed space or hollow, especially one in a wall for a statue, etc.

Developing a niche in the business world is really like carving out a reserved space for future customers by developing a solid reputation for quality, service and customer satisfaction.

Niching starts with just one customer who is satisfied with you and your product or service. It has been proven that any one satisfied business client, can directly influence as many as 250 individual decision makers as to whether they would use your services or not. Likewise those 250 individuals could influence up to 62,500 other people in the a similar manner. The numbers here are just staggering, aren't they?

In the real world one satisfied customer is not going to give you 250 leads out of the goodness of his heart. You have to earn your client's trust and you have to ask, yes, ask for their help in the form of testimonial letters, contact names and any other pertinent information.

- Successful companies or individuals always strive to sell to a number of diverse companies. They tend to build their clientele from a varied industrial or consumer base. By so doing, they avoid depending on a specific market segment for continued growth. They develop a niche in as many business sectors as possible.

- Successful companies are always looking to develop a niche with new market clients, who at first glance, would appear not to be a normal fit. They develop business with clients who have never even thought of using their specific product or service.

- Successful companies develop innovative niche markets in areas such as fund raising or special promotional concept accounts.

Whenever you discover a company that has developed a niche in a number of unique business applications for it's products, you will find a company that has an ability to design tailored marketing plans that are as diverse as the companies with whom they do business.

Companies with several market niches, without exception, have a commonality in their marketing strategy. The commonality of which we speak, is that adherence to the quality and integrity of the line dictates every marketing strategy that they employ in both written and verbal communications.

How To Open Doors Through Cross-Selling Methods

Many salespeople receive a rejection and close the door forever on a what was once a prospect. They fail to look ahead and take that one extra step towards the prospect that could mean the difference between success and failure.

Suppose you are selling computer systems. At the time of the phone call the prospect is very firm that they will not be in the market for computer systems for at least two years or more. They refuse to see you or the salesperson for that area. End of call?

On the contrary. Your phone discovery is just beginning. The prospect has already indicated that he does, in fact, use computer systems in his operation. Wouldn't it be logical to switch gears and ask for the opportunity to quote on the service of his equipment? One hook, that could be used is as follows:

If we could raise your uptime, and lower your downtime, could we get together sometime?

You might ask what servicing a competitor's equipment has to do with the selling of new equipment? Well, it has everything to do with it. First of all, if your service people land a contact with the prospect, they will obviously get to know the key decision-makers in the company. They will know exactly what kind of equipment the company employs, as well as the shortcomings of that equipment in handling certain requirements.

Your service people will also be in a position to advise the prospect precisely when it is no longer feasible to continue the maintenance of older equipment. The feedback from the service personnel gives the sales department the inside track on when to launch a sales offensive and exactly what kind of equipment to recommend. Wouldn't you really start the race from the pole position as opposed to starting from the back of the track? Of course you would.

Conversely, if you are in the service business and are focusing on securing additional service business, it will obviously be to your benefit to be versatile enough to switch into the sales mode if the conversation is leaning in that direction. The rule of thumb to follow is to never say no to any request, even if it means that you will have to source a specific product or unique service to satisfy the client.

Although this approach initially may not prove to be lucrative, you have opened the door to new prospects by illustrating that you care about their business. You will, indeed, receive your just reward sometime in the future.

Rather than just trying to hit a home run the next time you phone a prospect, try instead to just get on base. You will score a lot more runs by trying this approach.

How to Convert Those Not Interested Prospects Into Clients with Creative Selling Methods

After receiving the initial not interested response, you might want to respond with the following questions:

Would you be interested if…

Could I get your valued opinion on our product offering?

Could I get your advice on where my product would best fit?

Could I ask for your help?

After each of the aforementioned statements, assure the prospects that you will not waste their time.

If a meeting is still not possible, but the client has left the door open for you to call back in three to six months, use these procedures to stay in touch without being officious.

Place the prospect's name on your e-mail list and release special product offerings on a regular basis. Any correspondence should be personally addressed. Develop a company newsletter and mail or e-mail to key prospective accounts as well as your regular clients. The contents of the newsletter should have mass appeal to every industrial sector and could cover topics ranging from industry trends to new product developments to health and safety issues.

Invite your prospects to participate in the newsletter and ask for their response to the various topics covered. If communicating via e-mail, use a box format so that the client may simply check off that subject matter that they would like to see addressed.

You could also use the box format to invite the client to request a non-committal visit from any of your various departments.

If you are searching for new distributors, win their confidence over by providing detailed information on your planned advertising campaigns and how that campaign will assist them in the successful integration of your product line with theirs.

Be specific. Enclose a copy of your basic advertising strategy for the prospect to scrutinize. Use the following headings, accompanied by basic information and facts that will be covered under those headings.

Example of An Advertising Strategy Print Out

Factors Bearing on Creative Strategy - General

- General theme statement e.g. summer and fun and (your product) go together.

- Advertising will run from ----- to -----

- Industry and/or government approvals

- your product offers honest value

- Where your product is available (prospect's name mentioned here)

- Description of product i.e. descriptive interesting names (list)

Role Of Advertising

- To generate instant awareness and/or immediate traffic

- Long term image building campaign that will benefit all distributors (specify media to be used)

Creative Strategy

- To demonstrate why your product can benefit the consumer, what makes your product different and why your target market would purchase your product.

Benefit Support

- Why your product is so special?

- Availability of your product - continuity of supply

- Stress that your distributors offer one of the best selections anywhere

Tone of Advertising

(a)   Consumer

-       Fun, special, excitement

-     Magical

(b)   Business

If aimed at a more serious business market you might stress:

-       Sincerity, cost efficiency, lower maintenance costs, increased profits etc.

Target Audience

(a)   Consumer

-       Mention male or female

-       Specific age groups

-     The types of people. For example, people who like to do things a little out of the ordinary when they can, whether that be individually, as a family, or as a group (neighbours, friends etc.)

(b)   Business

The types of industry that would be attracted to your offering. Be specific. The type of company that is most apt to use your product or service.
It is wonderful to communicate with prospects, whether it be in the form of e-mail or verbal communication; however, unless you reach out by phone and make direct contact, your efforts will all be reduced.

It is critical that your salespeople follow up on all e-mail or written communication efforts within three to five business days. Most important, they should be prepared to ask the prospect for an honest, direct assessment of the contents of the communication. The nature of the call and the tone of voice should be devoid of any pressure.

Another effective approach in keeping touch with prospective clients is to invite them to free seminars.

A low key, no pressure approach should be used by the sales department in order to reassure prospects that they are under absolutely no obligation to make any commitments. Once again, the salesperson should contact those prospects that attended the seminar in order to get a true assessment of their value of the seminar from the prospect's viewpoint. What better approach to use as a market survey than to get the decision maker's opinions.

Whatever approach you use in order to stay in touch with prospective clients, you can rest assured that the old buzz words of the past are now obsolete. They have been replaced by words such as unique, quality, solutions, and cost-effectiveness.

The future rests with those companies that encourage cooperative professionalism and work towards a partnership in business. These business partnerships of tomorrow will be formed around old values such as trust, honesty, integrity and full service.

VII.   HOW TO DEVELOP TOP PRESENTATION SKILLS

Developing Good Questioning Skills

You can be the greatest announcer in the world but without good questioning skills you will only be able to achieve 15% - 20% of your sales potential.

Let's take a look at how to develop good questioning skills.

As mentioned earlier in the course, one method of handling the initial rejection is to simply ask why? By using this one word question you will rock prospects back on their heels and force them to reveal their real objections for not seeing you or buying your product. It is, after all a fair question to ask, isn't it? It is a direct response that demands a straight forward answer.

Although some people consider this approach to be too brash and forward, it does work. If you are too afraid and timid to ask the "why" question you are only going to limit your own chances of success. The prospect was bold enough to give you a straight forward no to your proposal. Can't you summon up enough courage to offer a like response? What have you got to lose? Absolutely nothing! What have you got to gain? Everything!

You will be absolutely astounded to hear the responses that you will receive in response to the "why" question. Most responses will be worded in such a manner that serve to extend the conversation. Lame-duck answers such as affordability are common. How does the prospect know this when we haven't even discussed the price? You have learned however, that price is an issue and proceed accordingly.

Another typical response is a statement by the prospect that he is locked into a contract. At least this statement leads to another immediate question on your part. Ask when the contract up for renewal? If it is within twelve months, suggest an introductory meeting to make the prospect's acquaintance.

Many prospects respond to the "why" question by emphasizing that they are satisfied with their present supplier. This statement indicates that the present supplier is doing a reasonably good job. Do you thank the prospect for his time and hang up? Of course not!

One response would be to emphasize that your company carries a few specialized items that the present supplier does not handle! Indicate that you are not trying to supplant his present supplier, but simply augment the present supplier's already extensive line or service.

The aforementioned responses were presented as a simple exercise to illustrate how you can to extend cold call conversations and turn those seemingly lost calls into fruitful calls.

Other follow up questions to ask in qualifying a prospect after you have received a poignant response to the "why" question would be as follows:

- Does the prospect plan a purchase within the next 12 months?

- Does the prospect have the potential in the near future that would lead them to seek your services?

- Is the prospect now, or in the near future, planning to upgrade the product or service that you are offering?

- Does your product or service even remotely offer a fit for the prospect's business requirements?

- Does the prospect appear to understand exactly what product or service you are offering?

In addition to asking questions of the prospect you must mentally be answering a number of your own questions during the course of the conversation.

- Is the prospect sincere and reasonably communicative?

- Do you personally feel that the prospect would truly benefit from your services?

- Does this company appear to have growth potential?

- What is the state of the industry in which this company would be categorized?

- Is the prospect willing to set a firm time and date to see you?

- Does the prospect appear to be open to new and innovative ideas?

- What personality type is the individual to whom you are speaking?

Good questioning skills will allow you to approach the prospect from an entirely different perspective from the one on which you had originally based your presentation. The development of good questioning skills will open up a whole new opportunity to learn about prospects' needs, providing you listen carefully to what they have to say.

Let's take a closer look at how to become a good listener.

Learning How To Become A Good Listener

Most salespeople are so intent on getting the appointment or making the sale, that they try to curtail the prospect's conversation. By so doing, they may pass up the opportunity to learn about key factors that quite conceivably could affect the type of sale, the size of the sale, and, in fact, whether or not they even make the sale.

A lift truck representative spoke to a prospect on the phone about materials handling equipment. The prospect's first reaction was to inform the salesperson that the business was operated out of a two story building and that the space available was so limited that they couldn't even think about utilizing lift equipment.

Rather than let the conversation end there, the salesperson offered several possible solutions without success. The prospect, who seemed to appreciate his concern, admitted that the business had outgrown the present premises and that the company was considering the purchase of a larger facility. The prospect told the salesperson to call back in six months, at which time a decision would have to have been made.

The salesperson noted the date in his call back in his database and called back faithfully, as instructed. Lo and behold the company had in fact purchased a new building after 15 years of renting the former outdated facility, and required logistics planning assistance for their brand new warehouse. The salesperson sold them one electric forklift truck, followed by two more electric units within 6 months. Total value of the sale was over $40,000.00.

The moral of the story is to never stop trying to be of assistance and to listen for key words or implications of future developments. Once the salesperson got the prospect to talk, he let the prospect sell himself on his own requirements without interruption.

By listening carefully, the salesperson learned that this business was successful, that their present warehousing was not at all cost efficient, and that they were thinking about a progressive move. Every statement that the prospect made was a buying signal.

Another important listening skill worth developing is the ability to detect the health of the prospect's business by listening to their tone of voice.

If the tone of voice is generally upbeat and the prospect indicates even a remote interest in the subject on which you are talking, it is an obvious signal that you should and would continue to pursue the subject matter.

Conversely, if the decision maker's voice is the epitome of despondency and indicates that their business or industry is rapidly sliding into oblivion, it is obvious that to continue the conversation would be an exercise in futility. Don't waste time on the losers. There are thousands of winners out there to pursue.

A word of caution. If you have the slightest doubt that you are misreading the prospect's mind set, put your doubt to rest by asking what it would take to turn the prospect's business around.

Listen carefully for the prospect's response and relate that response directly to the product or service that you are offering. Ask yourself this question: "Will my product or service honestly help this prospect revitalize his flagging business? "You are the only person that can provide an answer to your own question.

Many sales people hear what the prospect is saying but don't listen. They hear that the prospect is not buying now, but fail to listen and capitalize on buying signals.

Many sales people are so anxious to make a sale TODAY, that they forget about tomorrow and let the real prospects slip through their fingers.

If the prospect voluntarily mentions the possibility of landing a contract in 6 months that will create a need for your particular services - that is a true buying signal.

Do you make a note to call the prospect back in 6 months? If you do so, chances are you'll be too late! You should make an appointment to see the prospect as soon as possible, before your competition has the same opportunity to get to know the prospect personally and to learn more about their business. You will be better able to meet their needs by becoming more knowledgeable than your competition.

Probably the most important listening skill that you can develop is the ability to read the response that you hear after posing the benefit, question, or hook, at the conclusion of a script.

If the prospect responds with a resounding yes, and you are confident that they fully understand the nature of your business, make the appointment and say no more. The prospect is obviously eager to meet with you.

The prospect who is hesitant, may not fully comprehend what your service is all about. The approach to take here is to simplify your service in as few words as possible. Once prospects volunteer information that confirms that they have a grasp of what your company offers, it is now up to you to instantly assimilate that information.

Your listening skills will dictate the final closing statement in the form of a question. How prospects answer that question should be a clear indicator of whether or not to proceed further.

Your judgement in determining the qualified lead from the unqualified will become fine tuned through constant practice at listening to the answers given to your own questions.

Regardless, of how adept you become at questioning and listening skills, it is virtually impossible to guarantee that every phone lead is a qualified lead. You will find however, that with experience, the number of unqualified leads will be substantially reduced.

One word of advice. It is a fatal mistake on the part of management to become obsessed with the quality of leads generated on the phone. No one can judge the quality of a lead but the salesperson who has that face to face meeting. Even then, if that salesperson does not have the necessary skills to uncover needs, it is unfair in many instances, to blame the lack of results on poor qualifying skills.

Developing Fact Finding Skills Through Phone Discovery

There are rare instances, due to extenuating circumstances, when it will be necessary for both the caller and the prospect to conduct a phone discovery in order to determine if a visit is appropriate. The purpose of such a discovery is to determine if the seller's product or service will be of potential benefit to the prospect. Many prospects insist on a briefing prior to a visit in order to maximize the efficient utilization of their time.

Conversely, if the prospect's place of business is located a great distance from that of the vendor, it is only prudent for the salesperson to pre-qualify the prospect through phone communication.

It is the responsibility of the salesperson to chair this phone discovery in a professional manner. Many prospects will want to establish why they should do business with your company and how your product or service will benefit their company both now, and in the future. The application of your product or service as you initially visualize it may have to be drastically altered in order to meet specific needs.

If you are to be successful, it is vital that you question prospects as to types and age of equipment or service that they presently use. Ask for the names of suppliers that they presently deal with and ask for what purpose the product or service is used. By asking questions you will be better able to present a proposal that makes sense.

Other important issues that must be discussed include the level of frequency that the product or service will be used. Does the company plan to expand in the near future, both in physical size and/or in the number of employees? Where does the company see itself going in 5 years or ten years? Has the company budgeted for anticipated growth? How much? Does the decision-maker have forward vision? Is the company likely to keep abreast of technological changes to meet changing needs?

Ask what goals the company has on the issues of personal training, health and safety, new product development, pay equity and so on? Where does the decision-maker feel that changes should be made in order to improve cost efficiency and profitability? What are the strengths of the company? What are the major weaknesses?

Obviously you won't have time to ask all the pertinent questions on the phone; however, by asking key questions on the major issues or requirements, you will at least be able to assimilate a logical presentation. At the time of the face to face meeting, you will then be able to concentrate on the greater issues or criteria, upon which you will base your final recommendations.

Last, but not least, are you talking to the right person? Does this person actually make the final decision? Some salespeople have been known to call on buyers for several years without knowing that their contacts could not make the final buying decision.

Is it any wonder that these salespeople have failed to get the business?

In summation, your sales results, both on the phone and in person will be a direct reflection of your ability to probe the prospect in a professional manner. By developing outstanding fact finding skills you will not be known by the client as the one-time sales sensation, who sold the wrong product, but rather as a leading authority who is trusted to look after all the client's future requirements in your specific field of endeavor.

Projecting The Local Authority Image For Your Company

When speaking to a total stranger on the phone, it is important that you project an image that you are the expert in your specific field of endeavor. Your voice and your statements indicate that you know your product/service inside out, that you are fully aware of what your competition can offer, and that you are familiar with the entire market place.

When speaking about the competition, be totally honest in discussing their strengths and weaknesses. Make certain that you have your facts straight before making any statement. If you are uncertain, admit your ignorance. A prospect will respect the honest person over someone who makes misleading statements.

The local authority image can also be embellished by mentioning names of prestigious clients with whom you have done business. Don't be shy about blowing your own horn.

If you don't sell yourself, nobody else will do it for you. It is critical that you achieve instant credibility by establishing that you, do indeed have a track record of success - and the references to back up that success. By making a statement that you have solved similar problems on an ongoing basis with other clients, you are instilling a feeling of confidence in the mind of the prospect.

If you feel that your service is a good one for the prospect, say so, but be prepared to back it up during your face to face meeting.

By projecting a local authority image you will open doors to unlimited opportunities. By proving that you are, in fact, the local authority, you will also be able to close the door on your competitors.

How To Reflect An Air Of Confidence That Wins Instant Respect

The confident salesperson is one who answers questions with a direct, honest answer without undue hesitation. The confident sales person does not use negative words such as may, if, possibly, sometime, but rather emphasizes positive words like can, will and now.

Sales people that are able to win respect make confident statements that any time spent on a presentation will prove to be of value to the prospect.

By making positive statements throughout the course of your conversation with the prospect, you are really saying that you have something valuable to offer the prospect, that you know your subject matter, and most important, you are not going to waste the prospect's time.

It is of great benefit to develop all the aforementioned statements and techniques; however, it is the voice alone that really carries the day. An actor can have the greatest lines in the world, but it is how those lines are delivered to the audience that determines success or failure.

In sales, the secret to success is to be able to speak with authority and to avoid the pitfall of speaking in a condescending manner. If the voice indicates even the slightest patronizing mannerism, you will have lost. Practice ending each statement with true conviction and avoid, at all cost, ending your statements in a tone of voice that indicates a question rather than a statement.

The rule of thumb is to speak to all levels, from the shipper to the president, in exactly the same manner and to never be intimidated by anyone, regardless of their status.

You and you alone, must develop your own level of confidence. It is an acquired skill that is only mastered through hours and hours of practice. Once you've got it, nobody can take it away from you. You will have acquired a skill that very few salespeople have ever bothered to master and it will truly elevate you above the rest of the crowd.

VIII.   HOW TO CLOSE THE APPOINTMENT

How to Close the Appointment

The number one skill that must be acquired before becoming a good closer is the development of opportunity recognition skills. This chapter is a natural extension of Chapter VI, How To Overcome Objections, and will provide you with all the firepower necessary to close the appointment.

Let's take a look at some of the excuses, or objections - as we mistakenly call them - and how we can turn them into positives through the development of opportunity recognition skills.

Imagine that you are speaking to a prospect or prospects right now, today. You have delivered the script in a professional manner and have used the original Hook with precise timing and expertise. Unfortunately, your script has met with rejection due to the following excuse statements.

Excuse Statement #1
In response to proposed sale of handling equipment:

We're moving into a new distribution facility. Call me back in 6 months.

Excuse Statement #2
In response to any sales scenario:

I have an open mind but your timing is bad. Call back in 12 months.

Excuse Statement #3
In response to any sales scenario:

I'm going on vacation. Call back in 10 days.

Excuse Statement #4
In response to a sales training call:

I'm initiating some organizational changes in our sales department. Call back in the new year.

Excuse Statement #5
In response to a sales training company call:

> I'm too busy hiring and training new sales people

Excuse Statement #6
In response to a warehouse equipment company sales call:

> We're reorganizing our warehouse. I haven't got 5 minutes to spare.

Excuse Statement #7
In response to any sales scenario:

> We're in our busy season. Call me in 2 months.

Excuse Statement #8
In response to any sales scenario:

> I'd like to talk but we can't afford it.

Excuse Statement #9
In response to a computer supplier call:

> No time. We're updating our entire computer system.

Excuse Statement #10
In response to any sales scenario:

> Send me literature and call me back.

There are enough excuses to fill a complete book. These ten statements are just a few of the most common excuses. Would you hang up the phone after hearing these? Ninety-five percent of salespeople do just that. That's a fact! Ninety- five percent of salespeople grant the prospect's wish to get rid of them - forever.

What opportunities did the prospect miss? Who knows? We'll never know, will we?

It is at this point that the real salesmanship begins. The prospects have responded with a reason why they can't see you. The ball is now in your court. The first step in returning the ball back to the other side of the court is learning how to quickly retrieve the positive aspects from a seemingly negative statement.

What did each of these statements have in common? The answer is that not one single statement had the word "no" in it. Does that tell you something?

Although everyone out there is selling a different product or service, there is a commonality in the reading of these statements. Each statement really does contain a buying signal if you listen closely. Let's take a closer look.

How To Recognize Buying Signals And Use Them To Close Early

Excuse Statement #1

This statement represents a new opportunity. It indicates a possible expansion of the present business. If you are selling warehouse related equipment, you can't wait 6 months. To do so would, in all probability, result in your competition getting the business.

You still have to act now! One suggestion is to offer the prospect your logistics planning expertise on a non-committal basis. Ask for a brief introductory meeting. Assure brevity and suggest that you will leave important information for the prospect to peruse.

Excuse Statement #2

This statement indicates that the prospect has a definite interest in your product or service. As far as bad timing is concerned, a good salesperson does not let timing, good, bad, or otherwise, interfere with the primary objective -to get the appointment. At this early stage in the conversation, you do not know what the prospect means by bad timing.

Go for the close early by suggesting that your meeting will be an introductory meeting only and that you will keep it brief. Guarantee the prospect that you will not waste valuable time. It will be time well spent.

Excuse Statement #3

The first thing to note here is that the prospect has left an opening. Your script has obviously been well received; however, 90% of its contents will be forgotten in ten days. You will have lost the element of surprise as well as the impact that your message created. What do you do now? Simple. Ask that the prospect to pencil in a tentative appointment now for a specific date and time after the scheduled vacation period. Send an e-mail to confirm.

Excuse Statement #4

If changes are taking place, the timing is perfect to possibly work with the decision maker during the transition period. It presents a golden opportunity to lay groundwork for a fresh start in the area of sales development.

Ask for a brief meeting in order to leave valuable information that will assist the decision maker in the organization's planning process.

Excuse Statement #5

An opportunity statement. You don't want to let that one off the hook, especially if you are in the sales training business.

This prospect needs some help. The individual is too busy hiring and training people to do his own job. Perhaps he needs a sales manager or a marketing specialist. He definitely needs someone to teach training skills. If he is hiring personnel, it is a strong signal that business is growing and is healthy.

Suggest a very early AM or late PM meeting, even a Saturday AM appointment. Do what you have to do to get a face to face meeting, now. Stress the fact that you can assist in the hiring and training process and free up some of his valuable time to pursue other important matters.

Excuse Statement #6

The word "reorganizing" has several implications. This company could be expanding, downsizing or automating its facility. There could be need for computers, racking, lift trucks, hydraulics and a myriad of miscellaneous products.

Assure the prospect that you provide solutions that are cost effective and that will improve their bottom line. The right time for a visit is today.

Excuse Statement #7

If you are in the business of solving problems, the ONLY time to see a prospect is when business is at peak operation - particularly if the nature of the business is seasonal. It is during his peak period that certain deficiencies will obviously surface. Point out that now is the time to correct shortcomings prior to the next busy time period. An outsider is able to offer a whole new perception to problem solving that those on the inside would never even consider.

Assure brevity and get that all-important first meeting, if for only a 10 minute introduction.

Excuse Statement #8

At this stage, these types of prospects do not even know the cost of your product or service. They have a real fear of spending money. In such cases, salespeople must emphasize that their product/service can be tailored to any budget. Most important, it has to be stressed that the prospect will actually be saving money.

Stress the non-committal aspect of any meeting and make the appointment.

Excuse Statement #9

It is obvious from this statement that prospects such as this believe in keeping up to date, that they believe in their companies and that they are sold on becoming more cost efficient and productive. These prospects are not reluctant to spend money, if they are able to improve their operations' performance levels.

Assure these prospects that you understand the value of time and that you will not waste it. Emphasize that the meeting will be highly beneficial and that you can demonstrate exactly how your company will help save them thousands of dollars on computer supplies.

Excuse Statement #10

In this particular circumstance, remember that the prospect has not said no. The request for literature is a common ploy used to delay the decision making process.

State very firmly that you do have literature and that you would be most pleased to forward it to the prospect. You then turn the tables by stating that everyone's needs are different and that a face to face meeting would be best in determining the prospect's unique needs.

Suggest a meeting date be set now to discuss the offerings outlined in the information package that you have promised to send.

In each of the ten statements you have listened carefully to the prospects' statements, you have empathized with their situation and you have tried to close with very limited success.

The secret weapon for dramatically improving your closing ratio. It is called The Secondary Hook.

THE SECONDARY HOOK

How To Use The Secondary Hook To Get A Positive Response

The secondary hook requires the use of a soft approach, followed by a question that appeals to the prospect's sense of fairness. The question is worded such a manner so as to elicit a yes response. If the prospect says no to the secondary hook, he is made to look either foolish or ignorant. A no response will not only indicate a prospect's character, but will tell you up front that he is not, in fact, a prospect at all.

The secondary hook should be entirely different from the original hook that was employed, but should be directly related to it.

Let's look at a few secondary hooks that could be employed as they relate to the objection statements that we just completed.

Statement #1 (Moving into new facilities)
The approach:

You know, Ms. Prospect, one of our major areas of expertise is in the area of logistics planning.

The secondary hook:

If we could demonstrate precisely how we could design your facility to maximize productivity levels AND reduce costs, could we get together?

Wait for the response. Are mornings or afternoons best for you.' Close the appointment.

Statement #2 (Timing is bad. Call back)
The approach:

I have an idea, Mr. Prospect. Permit me to introduce myself and leave some pertinent information with you. It will be a brief introductory meeting only.

The secondary hook:

Is that a fair request? Wait for the response and then close the appointment.

Note: You are appealing to the prospect's sense of fairness. Would you say no to such a reasonable petition? I think not.

Statement #3 (Going on vacation. Call back)
The approach:

You know Ms. Prospect, we all have such a busy schedule these days, don't we? Could I make a suggestion?

The secondary hook:

I'll be in your area the week of ………… (after the prospect's vacation). Could you tentatively pencil me in for Monday, ……………… at 11:00 AM for a brief non- committal meeting?

Wait for the response and close the appointment. Repeat the date and time.

Note: You have asked several questions that almost demand a yes response. Once the yes is stated, it is usually not too difficult to get the prospect to agree to the final and most important question - the request for a meeting.

Statement #4 (Organization changes in sale department)
The approach:

That's very interesting, Mr. Prospect. We recently submitted a written discovery to XYZ Co. in town on that very subject. We are presently working with them on a contractual basis. One last question:

The secondary hook:

If we could help your company to build a sales organization that will meet or exceed any and all specific revenue targets, could we get together for 15 minutes? Wait for response.

Statement #5 (Too busy hiring and training new sales people)
The approach:

You certainly have a full plate, Ms. Prospect. It may interest you to know that we work closely with sales managers to enhance their position. Our program affords sales managers the time to concentrate their efforts in the business of sales development and management.

The secondary hook:

If we could custom design a sales training program that will ensure that your salespeople meet or exceed their targets, could we talk? or, If we could maximize individual sales results through specific direction and support, could we get together for 15 minutes?

Statement #6 (Reorganizing our warehouse. No time)
    The approach:

One of our services is to provide a free consulting service for improved warehouse management practice.

The secondary hook:

If we could initiate a program that would reduce handling costs and substantially increase profit, could we have just 15 minutes of your time?

Statement #7 (we're in our busy season)
    The approach:

I can appreciate how busy you must be at this time; however, our experience in seasonal industries has proven that this really is the prime time for a non-committal meeting. I'm sure you'll know in the first five minutes of our discussion if we can be of help to you.

The secondary hook:

If we could raise your uptime, lower your downtime, AND increase bottom line results, could we have 10 minutes?

Statement #8 (We can't afford it)
    The approach:

Our cost depends solely on the needs of the client. We are particularly sensitive to smaller companies and have designed cost-effective programs for that market.

The secondary hook:

If we could offer a program that is affordable, AND yields dramatic profit increases, could we visit for 15 minutes?

Statement #9 (No time. Updating computer system)
    The approach:

It certainly is a big job. What system are you installing?

The secondary hook:

We are the leading supplier of diskettes, paper and other accessories. If we could dramatically reduce your cost AND improve your image, could we spend 5 minutes to explain our unique program?

Statement #10 (Send literature)

The approach:

We would be pleased to send you literature; however as everyone's needs are so diverse, the information I send may not be applicable to your specific concerns.

The secondary hook:

If we could address you needs immediately and propose a no-obligation cost-effective solution, could we have 10 minutes of your time?

Discovering The Prospect's Real Objections

After you have used the secondary hook and received a direct response, the real objection or objections, may or may not surface. The very fact that prospects are still talking to you at this stage is a real sign of encouragement. Their concerns are important to them and thus should be important to you. Listen carefully to the prospects and do not interrupt until they have finished. It is surprising how much you can learn by listening.

With the current explosion of home based business consultants, many prospects have been burned in the past by so called experts whose performance was mediocre at best. They try to screen salespeople in order to save time. If you sense that credibility is the real objection, be prepared to face it head on. Provide the prospect verbally with past and present references and move forward with confidence to the close once again.

Many salespeople who are unsure as to what the prospect is objecting to are reluctant to ask a direct question in order to determine the real objection. This is a mistake. Make a positive statement to the prospect that you know he is interested in increasing profits or he would have terminated the conversation. Immediately following this statement. Ask why he is reluctant to meet with you for a few minutes? If the response to the question indicates a lack of interest in your product or service, period! hang up the phone - you've wasted enough time!

After all, there are hundreds of other calls you can make where good reason will prevail. If however, you get a logical, legitimate response that the present supplier already covers all the bases, you have something on which to hang your hat. At least now you know the real objection. In this case your response could point out that many of your best customers said the same thing until they saw what you had to offer. Tell the prospect that he will not be disappointed.

If the objection, as mentioned earlier - is one of credibility due to the fact that your company is not a household name, reassure the prospect again that you will provide names and phone numbers of clients at the time of your meeting.

There are really any number of real objections that could conceivably rise to the surface. The section on Overcoming Objections will assist you in responding to these real objections. Practice overcoming objections and excuses on a daily basis until they have become second nature. One word of caution. Do not get involved in a prolonged phone discussion or you're dead in the water.

Do not avoid answering questions, but rather keep your responses brief. After responding to several questions in a courteous manner, simply state that you will answer any and all questions that might arise at the time of the meeting. Never lose sight of your main objective - to get the appointment.

How To Depressurize a Tense Situation and Win Approval Using The Three E's

You've heard of the ABC's, now comes the three E's. No, the three E's are not a credit rating but rather a unique method of extricating yourself from a seemingly lost position to that of win-win situation.

The first E stands for Empathy. It means that you sympathize with prospects and listen to their concerns or tales of woe. You listen and respond to their problems like a member of their own family.

The Second E symbolizes the word Emphasis. You emphasize exactly how, when and where you can solve the prospect's problems. You emphasize support, understanding and commitment. Above all else, you emphasize success.

Last, but not least, the third E stands for Evacuate. After you have shown empathy and have emphasized how you can solve the prospect's problems, it is time to evacuate yourself from the conversation by winning approval to see that prospect.

How To Win Approval And Get The Appointment

You have impressed the prospect with your skill in holding his interest, in listening to his problems, and in imparting the knowledge of your specific area of expertise. However, it will all go for naught unless you get the appointment. It will be like a baseball pitcher who pitches 8 2/3 innings of no-hit baseball, only to have the 27th batter hit a home run to win the game for the opposing team.

There are a number of ways to ask for the appointment as already stated in the chapter dealing with the primary close and the secondary close. Following are some additional ideas on how to close the appointment.

- What day would be best to give you a brief overview - Monday or Thursday?

- If you are even remotely interested in increasing profits, a meeting will be well worth your time! Are mornings or afternoons better for you?

- I guarantee that the time spent with me will be worth it. Are mornings or afternoons best for you?

- If we are unable to prove our worth to you in the first 5 minutes of our conversation, you can terminate the meeting. Is that a fair request? Are mornings or afternoons better for you?

- I have an idea! Let's have a brief, non-committal introductory meeting to see if we have a fit. Is that a reasonable request? Are mornings or afternoons best for you?

For those prospects who appear to be intimidated when asked to make a commitment for a specific date and time, use the following approach:

I'll be in your area on Tuesday, Could I drop in at about 10:30 am to make your acquaintance and leave some literature?

In 9 cases out of 10, the prospect will agree to such an arrangement, and will advise you to call first. At the very least, you will have connected with a new prospect that you otherwise might never have met.

The next time you call, the prospect will be able to match the voice with the face, thereby dramatically increasing your chances of making a sale.

IX.   SECOND CALL FOLLOW-UP METHODS

Follow-Up Scripts

Assume that you are selling a sales training program. As selling an intangible is the most difficult challenge any salesperson could face in the selling business, the methodology that you will learn here is transferable to virtually any sales situation.

Let's set the stage for the theatrics by recapping what happened on the first attempt to get an appointment. An effective follow up script is then employed to close the appointment.

Script #1

Recap of original call: The prospect was sold on your service and asked that you call back to schedule a specific date and time. He had a legitimate reason for making such a request.

Follow-Up Script

Good ………… Mr. Prospect! My name is …………... I'm with ………… the sales development company. At the time of our last conversation, you asked that I call back this week to arrange a meeting with you regarding our sales development service. I have an opening on Monday or Friday. What day is best for you? Are mornings or afternoons best for you? Make the appointment and repeat the date and time.

Script #2

Recap of original call: The prospect absolutely refused to see you until she received a detailed overview of your company's service and a list of references. There was no guarantee that the prospect would grant you an appointment.

Follow-up Script

Good ………… Ms. Prospect! …………. I'm with ………. the sales development company. As you will recall, you requested an overview and references. I assume you received them. As you can see, we have an excellent track record. Just one question: If we could help your company to meet or exceed all you sales objectives, would you allow us to have just 15 minutes of your time? Are mornings or afternoons best for you? Make the appointment.

Script #3

Recap of original call: Your first phone call regarding sales training services got the appointment. During the initial meeting it was determined that your program did not fit the prospect's needs as you did not have a customer service module available at that time.

Follow-up Script

Good ………… Mr. Prospect! My name is …………… I'm with ………….. the sales development specialists. You'll be pleased to know that we have now developed an all new customer service module. It addresses all your concerns and encompasses all the basic selling skills needed to make your people successful at the retail level.

Just one question: If we could custom design a program that will substantially increase retail sales, could we get together? Are mornings or afternoons best for you? Make the appointment.

Script #4

Recap of original call from sales training company: At the time of the original call, this company did not have any outside representatives, but were in the process of hiring. The prospect insisted that you call back in a few months.

Follow-Up Script

Good …………… Ms. Prospect! My name is ……………… I'm with …………… As I recall, you were in the process of hiring 3 or 4 representatives for outside sales. Just one question: If we could enhance your product training with our proven sales skills program in order to maximize positive results, could we meet for a few minutes? Are mornings or afternoons best for you?

Script #5

Recap of original call: At the time of the original call, the prospect determined that he could not afford the service being offered. The interest was there, however; the lack of funds prevented the prospect from pursuing the matter.

Follow-Up Script

Good …………… Mr. Prospect! My name is ……………….. I'm with ………… You may recall our last conversation regarding sales training. I'm calling back today to give you some good news! Our company has introduced a series of Mini sales training seminars at the fraction of the cost of the full program. You have the option of selecting the workshop session or sessions that would best suit the individual salesperson's needs.

Just one question: If we could offer you a cost-effective program that will deliver immediate benefits, could we get together for a few minutes?

Script #6

Recap of original call: The Prospect, although indicating a sincere interest in your service, rejected the idea of a visit for undetermined reasons.

Follow-Up Script / Third Party Endorsement

Good .... Ms. Prospect! My name is .... I'm with a company called .... In reference to our previous conversation regarding sales training, I thought that you would be interested in learning that we just completed a program with   here in town. They have achieved a ..% increase in sales and are elated with the results.

Just one question: If we could offer some refreshing new ideas that would demonstrate precisely how we could help your company achieve similar sales gains, could we have a few minutes of your time?

Script #7

Recap of original call: The prospect indicated that he was satisfied with sales performance levels and that his people took one-day sales training courses on an irregular basis. He left the door open by suggesting that you call back later.

Follow-up Script

Good .... Mr. Prospect! My name is .... I'm with a company called .... You suggested that I follow up with you at a later date. Just a couple of quick questions. Is that okay? Are all your people meeting their targets? Do you have a method for measuring performance?

One last question: If we could custom design a program that will significantly increase your sales over a 30, 60 or 90 day time period, would you allow us a few minutes of your time'?

Every day, salespeople are losing clients because the salesperson gives up, fails to follow-up or lacks the creativity to adjust their offering to suit individual client needs. The scripts that you have just read reflect both imagination and creativity. They highlight words, phrases and benefits that perhaps were not previously emphasized. In some cases they met the original objection head on by offering innovative new ideas and solutions.

Naturally you will make certain changes in your follow-up scripts to best fit the product or service that you are offering. If you use the basic techniques that you have learned in The Call Wizard, you will become proficient at closing the appointment and creating hundreds of new opportunities that previously might have been lost.

How To Use Stored Information To Your Advantage

Most salespeople make the critical mistake of not entering notes in their database at the time of the first call. Their call backs are repetitious and completely fail to recognize the prospect's original concerns. The salesperson is visualized by the prospect as being uncaring, selfish and inept. Would you like to deal with someone like this person?

You will dramatically increase your chances of success if you detail any and all significant information that the prospect has passed on. The information could be of a personal or business nature. It is not necessary to enter a lengthy discourse after each call, but rather to recap a thought process or statement with a one or two word notation.

When calling back, most prospects will be simply amazed that you remember so many details from the previous conversation. Of course, you may not have remembered them - you simply made an entry and reviewed them prior to your call back. Wouldn't you be pleased if a salesperson asked how your trip to Washington went, or how you enjoyed your vacation, or if your wife has given birth to your first born yet?

The prospect would probably think you were clairvoyant, as in all likelihood, he wouldn't even remember telling you these things. You are indicating that you are a caring person. This prospect will now extend the same courtesy to you as you have accorded him. It's just common sense.

The exact same types of entries should be made for comments made pertaining to the business side of your conversation as well. Main objections should be noted, as well as names of present suppliers or competitors. You should also enter the exact date that you are to call back. Perhaps the company is reorganizing, upsizing or downsizing or even moving. Are they hiring or firing? Is their particular industry on the upswing or downswing?

What is the personality type of the prospect? Any pertinent little comment can loom very large when the time arrives to make your call back. How you use your stored information could very well determine your success or failure with any prospect.

Before you make that call back, you must ask yourself if the script fits what you are trying to accomplish and if you have addressed the prospect's objections determine the benefits that you are going to stress in order to achieve maximum impact. What hook are you going to use on closing in order to reinforce your presentation?

A carefully crafted script will maximize your chances to achieve your objective. Rehearse the script several times in order to become comfortable with it and deliver it with true conviction. Do your homework and you will reap the rewards.

How To Put The Prospect On The Spot

There really is a fine line to walk when endeavouring to extricate a positive response from a prospect who will not make a decision. There is a difference between being proactive and just plain offensive.

When speaking on the phone to a prospect and the conversation is going nowhere, try one of these methods to put the prospect on the hot seat. The first method is to use a repeat hook or hooks that demand a "yes" response. After making one specific statement, you might ask the prospect if he is truly interested in increased profits. If the response is positive, ask for the appointment.

If the prospect continues to question as to how you are going to reduce their costs and increase profits, listen intently; respond in as few words as possible that you are going to introduce a monitoring system that will precisely demonstrate your approach.

If there is still reluctance on the part of the prospect stress again that you will not waste the prospect's time and that he can terminate the meeting after 5 minutes if he feels that you can't be of service!

Then comes the final hook that appeals to the prospect's sense of reason. You simply ask – in the form of a question – if the request you have made is fair.

The third method in putting the prospect on the spot is to create doubts in the prospect's mind that all is not as well within their company as they think it might be.

If, for example, you are selling sales training services, you might ask questions such as:

How do you measure performance?

Are all your people meeting their targets?

Do your people service existing clients or go after new business?

Are you saying that you're not interested in a 10% sales increase?

By asking pointed questions such as these, you have tweaked the prospect's interest.

They now will probably want to find out how the professionals really do measure performance and why all their salespeople are not meeting their targets. They are probably also wondering about new accounts. It could be that there haven't been any in a few months. And finally, who wouldn't be interested in a 10% sales increase?

Once the prospect is softened-up with some heavy questions, you can move right in for the appointment.

Use and reuse what works best for you, but don't be afraid to ask several times for the appointment, if that's what it takes.

Be persistent, be polite and always be professional.

Recapping Your Previous Presentation Using the Three R's Approach

Recalling

If you have delivered a sound script to your prospect - and have projected the local authority image with the utmost confidence - the prospect will undoubtedly remember your call. By employing your usual introduction, the prospect will have instant recall of the nature of your business.

The next step is up to you. You now have to take the initiative by reviewing the exact nature of the prospect's concerns or objections in as few words as possible. By so doing, you will make an instant impression with all prospects. The next step in this logical sales sequence is to develop relating skills that build trust with the prospect.

Relating

Relating skills are really the development of an innate ability to listen, to sympathize, and to offer real assistance in a low key manner that wins respect. One of the most important skills you can develop - and it only comes from experience - is the ability to relate one prospect's specific problems with that of an actual client who has had similar problems.

You paint a clear picture in words that illustrate how you developed a lasting solution for your client. You provide the name of the company and a contact at that company who will vouch for your ability to get results. The third and final stage in the relating process is the reinforcement of your overwhelming desire to be of service.

Reinforcing

The verb "reinforce", according to the dictionary means to give new force or strength to. If you have done your homework, you will have passed the recalling and relating stages with flying colours. You have already reinforced your position with the prospect. The final reinforcement must come from within, and should reflect all the strength that you built-up through an impassioned plea for a follow-up meeting.

The final reinforcement plea should not deviate from the suggested format; however, the wording of this reinforcement hook will obviously be different from any that you have used before with this client.

Two examples of a reinforcement hook might be as follows:

a)	Tangibles

If we could guarantee that you will receive the quality, the price and the continuity of supply as discussed, could we have your authorization?

b)	Intangibles

If we could initiate a strategic plan that will dramatically increase cash flow and profit, could we spend a few minutes with you?

Use your own words and phraseology. But most important, act out your script with conviction, passion, and confidence that unequivocally states that you are the expert and that you are successful. You will overcome any and all obstacles, and, you will win approval.

How to Freshen-Up Your Previous Presentation

If your company is progressive in nature, it will constantly be developing new programs to meet the needs of the ever changing marketplace. Perhaps you have new promotions to discuss or possibly are launching new products. Any new idea that you have developed offers a new opportunity to revitalize your presentation to any prospect with whom you have had previous contact.

Here's an example of how you can rekindle the interest of a prospect when calling, for example, on behalf of a sales training company.

The opening and closing statements that you will employ remain basically the same. It is the main body of the script that changes in order to reflect a brand new program that is intended to capture the imagination of my audience. The new message might state that your company has have developed a number of new programs or modules that accommodate virtually every training requirement or application.

This new approach says everything, but says nothing. It is intended to pique the prospect's sense of curiosity without giving specifics. The specifics will be discussed in detail, only if a face to face meeting can be arranged.

Another very important method that can be used effectively in creating a fresh approach is the creation of an entire new imagery through word substitution. People form images in their mind's eye by relating descriptive words to the desired results that they want to achieve. Even if your phone presentation is bereft of any startling new ideas, you can make it appear new by introducing different key words or phrases that will achieve the desired impact. Let's look at a few examples.

The word dramatic is changed to significant or substantial. Increased profits becomes bottom line results. Daily sales increases can be described as increased cash flow. Innovative new ideas becomes, creative new ways. Increased warehouse productivity now reads as increased uptime and lower downtime.

The list goes on and on. Use your imagination to create your own new imagery. The combinations that can be employed are really only limited by your own imagination.

How to Use Referrals To Bolster Your Credibility

The use of the referral system is probably more effective in some sales situations than in others. It is, however; an effective tool that you can employ when the opportunity presents itself While many company executives are reluctant to give you a referral list to call on due to the competitive nature of their businesses, others are only too willing to offer their assistance.

Those that are willing to help you promote your product or service are generally manufacturers who depend mainly on distributors to sell their product. Rather than feeling threatened, they welcome the opportunity to be able to offer their distributors the benefit of your expertise. If their distributors are able to improve their overall performance levels, the improved results will benefit all parties. It is a win-win situation.

In direct sales - such as the real estate, automobile or insurance businesses - referrals are an integral part of the sales process. Satisfied customers are generally more than happy to pass on names of friends and neighbours who they feel could benefit from a specific product or service.

Whatever your situation may be - regardless of your product or service - there is a common logical sales sequence that should be adhered to in developing an effective script and phone presentation. It is important to remember that although you have been referred to a prospect, it does not mean that you will automatically close the sale by just picking up the phone.

In many cases, a referral call is a more difficult sell than a cold call, The point here is that a referral call must take nothing for granted. A complete script, spoken with the same conviction as any other call, must be delivered if you are to be successful.

The Mechanics of the Referral Script

The basics of the referral script should remain almost identical to your regular script. Following your opening statement, you might want to insert a brief mention of the person and the name of the company from whom you received the referral. A word of caution here. Make absolutely certain that you have pronounced both the individual's name and the company name correctly.

An incorrect pronunciation of name gives the impression that you have never really developed a close business relationship with either the referring individual or their company. This assumption on the part of the prospect is probably correct and your credibility will instantly vanish.

The fact that you have received a referral does not guarantee that you will be considered for any business opportunity. It is, therefore; important to act out your script in your normal manner and leave nothing to chance.

The main body of your presentation will state the type of service you provide, and the benefits that can be expected. It is at this point in the conversation that a personal referral can be used as a testimonial to your expertise. A brief statement, for example, that you were able to increase Axis's sales by 12%, will greatly enhance your chances of getting a fair hearing with the prospect.

In summation, if you want to bolster your credibility through the use of referrals remember to remain humble and tell the truth Do not assume the sale

Treat the referral client as you would any other cold call and close as early as possible.

X.   HOW TO MANAGE YOUR TIME

Organizing Your Call Backs

It is of critical importance to develop a computerized tracking system that tells you precisely when to follow up with a prospect. You've taken the time to make that initial cold call and have made some progress. Why waste it?

If you are also using a manual record system, transfer all you call backs and accompanying pertinent information - including those prospects that you were unable to reach - from your sales call sheets onto separate record sheets and file by salesperson and scheduled call each day. This should be done an a daily basis without fail. The exact procedure should also be followed if you have a computer entry tracking system.

Many salespeople do not adhere to a methodological system. If you fall into this lackadaisical category you are inviting mass confusion and are letting important prospects fall through the cracks on a daily basis. This system, simply put, does not work.

Prospective clients - despite the high volume of calls they receive - remember more detail than most salespeople give them credit for remembering. The highly organized prospects are also very cognizant of their own itinerary and resent receiving a second solicitation at a time other than the date that they had suggested for a call back. Conversely, busy executives are most impressed by salespeople who can follow directions and who call back on the day or week as requested by the prospect.

These salespeople have already achieved some degree of respect, as they have shown themselves to be considerate, diligent and highly organized. They have portrayed the image of professional salespeople who indulge in sound business practices. It is this type of salesperson who will turn a prospect into a client.

In summation,. plan your call backs in advance and rotate those unreachable prospects in a logical daily sequence in your database until you succeed in tracking each and every one of them down.

One final word of advice. Leave the easy or resold calls until the end of the day. (Those prospects that had previously agreed to meet with you, but were unable to commit themselves at the time of the call.)

By leaving the resold or guaranteed appointments until the end of the day, you have that all-important psychological advantage in knowing that your day will be successful, regardless of the outcome of the balance of your cold calls. If you can bank a number of these pre-sold call backs each day, your task in generating new appointments will be made much easier.

Experience shows that if the writing-up of the pre-sold calls is performed at the beginning of the day, the salesperson tends to slacken off a little and loses that extra edge in making what is normally the required number of calls necessary to meet the quota of appointments.

It really is possible to have your cake and eat it too. If, for example, you are able to secure four appointments from 9:00 am until 3:00 pm, and then cash in your pre-sold appointments, you will, indeed, have had an exceptional day.

If you can discipline yourself to work in the recommended manner as described, everyday will be an exceptional day.

Focusing on the Completion of One Task at a Time

Most salespeople or independent business people make the fatal mistake of trying to do too much at once. They combine daily appointment call efforts with outside sales and servicing duties, chase down accounts receivables and attend to numerous other tasks that may arise during the course of their normal daily routine.

If you are one of those people who tries to be Mr. or Mrs. Everything to Everyone, your appointment call efforts are doomed to failure. Why? you might ask. Well, first of all, any sales effort requires a high level of energy and consistency in order to be successful. A smooth rhythm of delivery must be achieved and then maintained on every call if you are to make an impact.

Interruptions will disrupt your timing and rhythm. If your appointment marketing campaign is to be successful, you must be prepared to make a great number of calls to achieve a minimal amount of success. You must also spend the time to plan and organize your call backs throughout the day. Although everyone's success rate on a per call basis will vary, appointment call marketing is really a numbers game.

Last - but not least - with the advent of voice mail it is imperative that you remain completely focused on just making the correct contact. You could conceivably, find it necessary to make six (6) or more calls to a voice mail box before getting a live response. If you are counting on a prospect returning your voice mail message, forget it. It seldom occurs.

To sum up this section on focusing, successful appointment call marketing is the direct result of uninterrupted dedication. Nothing less will do. If you have designated two full days to appointment calls, do not allow anything to distract your efforts.

How To Organize Your Appointment Call Program /Outside Sales Ratio

Whether you are doing your own appointment calling or plan to hire someone to do it for you, here are some specific guidelines to follow:

Appointment Call Days

Set aside two consecutive days in the week that are completely dedicated to the appointment call function. These two days should be the same two days every week. Two consecutive days are recommended, as the first day is basically a warm-up day-an opportunity to tune up your script and develop a sense of rhythm.

This first day sets the stage for those all important call backs on the second day, when you will be able to close in on the actual decision- maker whom you might not have known even existed prior to your first day's call. There is also a strong possibility that the decision-maker was not available at the time of your call. You have, perhaps, learned the name of, or were referred to, the decision-maker by either a superior or a subordinate of the decision-maker.

You've got to strike while the memory of the referring party, as well as your own retention abilities, are at their peak.

A second reason for dedicating two consecutive days to the appointment call function is the simple, but important matter of increased confidence levels. In addition to having honed your abilities at overcoming objections, you have managed to secure several appointments and ended the first day on a positive note. You now have the confidence to build on that success.

Time Planning For Appointments

Set your appointments at least one week in advance. By so doing, you will have allowed yourself some breathing room to attend to other important business matters and to prepare for the upcoming appointments with the prospective clients. Block off full days or half days on your calendar, in order to reserve time for specific tasks or obligations to which you are already committed. Make sure to update your calendar on a daily basis.

Confirm All Appointments

Confirm every single appointment. With today's business climate and accompanying pressures, a prospect's plans can change on a daily basis, so do yourself a favor and call ahead or send an e-mail to confirm. By getting into this habit, you will save yourself valuable time and money.

Planning Your Appointments Geographically

Given the cost of doing business in our highly competitive marketplace, try to reduce travel times and the accompanying costs by working smarter. It does not make good sense to set an appointment in the east end of a sprawling major city for 9:00 am and another appointment in the extreme west end of the same city for 10:30 am.

Always make it personal policy to blueprint a coverage plan by geographical area and to stay on course until the successful completion of that plan.

How To Prioritize Your Time

In an earlier chapter it was suggested that you make a list of both primary and secondary markets for your specific product line or service. Allocate 80% of your time to developing primary markets and 20% of your efforts to pursuing secondary markets. It is the development of the primary markets that will create the necessary cash flow as well as those all important referrals to assist you in pursuing secondary markets and special concept accounts.

One question often asked is: What days are best for cold calling? The answer is that no one day is better than another.

Your success on any given day is really a case of mind over matter. If you are totally professional and remain dedicated to the task, day-in and day-out, the results will be fairly equally balanced for each day of the week. You will get out of each day exactly what you put into it.

Once you have established your inside day(s) and outside day(s), do not change them around to accommodate present clients or for that matter, even to address your own personal needs. Discipline is the key to lead generation continuity. Continuity in strictly following a program will eventually foster success in achieving all goals that you might set for yourself.

Prioritize your time in a manner that allows some flexibility, but that also requires some honest discipline. Know exactly what your objectives are and don't veer off course until you achieve them.

XI.   DEALING WITH TECHNOLOGICAL CHANGE

How to Deal With Voice Mail and Use it To Your Advantage

Voice mail - although convenient and helpful to many individuals - represents an irritant to others. Regardless of your personal feelings on the subject, it is here to stay. We must learn to live in harmony with voice mail and other technological changes or perish.

As there will be certain times when it will be necessary for you to face voice mail head on, let's examine a number of approaches that can be employed. The obvious reason for leaving a message in a voice mail box is to create enough interest to insure that the prospect will call you back. There is a real art in how you word your message, how you deliver the message and how you close your message.

The Type of Message You Should Leave in a Voice Mail Box

It is important, when leaving a message, that you design a script that mentions the benefits and the positive results that prospects can expect to receive. The secret is to portray an image that you really want to offer unselfish service to prospects in terms of their needs, concerns, and objectives. You don't want to be portrayed as a high pressure salesperson out to make a quick buck.

An example of an effective voice mail script might be as follows (after initial introduction): Our mission is to **dramatically** increase your uptime and reduce your downtime. Just one question: If we could demonstrate **exactly** how we could raise your profits AND lower your production costs, would you allow me just 30 seconds of your time? Pause for a few seconds and then add: Thank-you for your courtesy in returning my call. I can be reached at ....

Now that's a message that just might capture the attention of a production manager, especially if the manager has recently been told by his superiors to reduce downtime and trim costs.

The Delivery of The Message

Although you are not speaking to the prospect live, it is very important to set out your script with the same degree of enthusiasm as is your normal habit. Words such as: dramatically, increase, reduce, raise etc. should be emphasized to maximize the impact of their intended meaning. The delivery of your message should be handled as if you are doing a professional commercial in a recording studio for airing at a later date.

Act like a professional announcer, sound like a professional announcer and you will be received like one.

How to Ensure That the Prospect Will Call You Back

There are no guarantees in life except death and taxes, however; your chances will be greatly enhanced if you avoid certain pitfalls.

The most common error that salespeople make when leaving a message is to generalize. They fail to offer one simple benefit. For example, a statement that you'd like to drop by to see if the prospect has any requirements is useless. The immediate reaction is – no reaction.

What is really wrong with this call? you might ask. It appears that the caller just wants to sell product for the sake of personal benefit. The call totally lacks any imagination, and certainly offers no specific customer benefits. The salesperson has not even tried to differentiate their company from the other competitors.

The message really gives no justifiable reason to take any type of action. Here is an example of a highly effective voice mail message:

Hello ……….. I'm with ………….. I'm calling to announce the launch of the most functional and driver friendly lift truck ever developed.

Please call me at your earliest convenience for details. I'll keep it brief! I look forward to your call.

Thank you for your courtesy. I'll be in the office until noon today. Leave your name and phone number.

Following are some additional ideas that will help you to improve the quality of your messages.

1.   Don't try to sell your product/service on the message

Try instead to offer a conceptual idea that will offer potential benefits to the prospect. The initial response to a salesperson who makes a run-of-the-mill sales statement that he would like to talk to you about sales training services, is inviting rejection. The prospect reacts in a normal manner by deleting the message.

On the other hand, if that same person is able to articulate thoughts and is able to indicate a specific idea or ideas as to how the prospect can meet or any sales volume targets, he will sit up and take notice. If someone calls who can help his sales people achieve the desired results, and make him look good in the eyes of his superior, he's going to extend him the courtesy of at least hearing that person's presentation. People will respond to you if they feel that there is a real opportunity to gain something from you.

2.   Do not detail benefits on the phone.

Once you've been instructed to start your message, use language that implies a face to face meeting is always best. Promise to answer all questions and cover details at the time of your meeting. The idea is to pique the prospect's interest to such an extent that they will want to call you back for more details.

3.   Do not let your frustration or anxiety show through when leaving the message.

Speak into a voice mail box in exactly the same manner as you would if the prospect was speaking to you live. Use exactly the same enthusiasm, inflection and emphasis as is your normal practice. Be very careful not to convey even the slightest trace of frustration at being unable to reach the prospect.

4.   Customize your message script to fit specific prospect objectives.

Develop enough scripts to give you flexibility with different prospects. The introduction could remain basically the same, the main body or benefit statement could be interchangeable, one script with another, as could your closing Hook. Enter the script you used on the voice mail message so as not to repeat it during the live conversation. The development of versatility in the area of script acting will prove to be a real asset to you, as it indicates that you are creative in your thinking, and can offer fresh new ideas. It will set you above the normal run-of-the-mill, phone sales people who lack colour, imagination and courage.

5.   Message Repetition and Courtesy

In closing your message, speak very deliberately when leaving your name, company name, and phone number. Repeat the same information a second time by slowly stating your name, the company you represent and your phone number.

Last, but most important, thank the prospect for extending you the courtesy of returning your call.

Preparing for the Voice Mail Message Call Backs

Now that you have optimized changes that the prospect will call back, you must obviously prepare yourself for the anticipated return call. People often receive call backs from prospects who just give their name and expect you to initiate a conversation. How do you remember why you called that individual and what was discussed on the voice mail message?

It can be very embarrassing to suffer a memory lapse when prospects have extended you the courtesy of returning your call. They do not understand that you make possibly a hundred calls in a given day, nor do they care. Prospects expect to be treated with importance.

The solution to the memory problem does not lie in taking a memory course, or in cultivating a photographic memory. You have to develop a system that gives you total recall. Try this system:

Enter data for every call on your program screen or call back form. For those calls where you left a message on voice mail, develop your own hieroglyphics such as "VM/LM/CB". Translated, these letters mean that you received a voice mail greeting (VM), left a message (LM) and will call back (CB) if you do not receive a response in two hours or less. You don't have to necessarily use these symbols. Use whatever works best for you. Record one word reminders of your objectives. Every fifteen or thirty minutes call up your program screen or check the call form to refresh your memory as to the names of individuals and companies from whom you expect a call.

When one of these VM individuals calls, refer immediately to your notations. You will immediately be aware of why you had called and exactly what you wanted to discuss. Thank the caller for returning your call and go right into your presentation. The caller or prospect will be impressed with your spontaneity and will listen intently to what you have to say.

This system will work.

Last Resort Measures to Find the Voice Behind the Voice Mail Box

If you are a top salesperson, you are, in all probability an ace "sleuth" as well. You don't give up until you track down that voice behind the voice mail – even if it takes weeks or even months. Following are some ideas that will assist you in your tracking endeavours

Don't be afraid to leave several messages at the same extension. Through repetition you are illustrating very emphatically that you are serious. Have the party that you are trying to reach paged. Be assured, it is the most effective way to reach the decision-makers..

Ask the receptionist if the party you are trying to reach is physically in the building. If the answer is no, try to determine the anticipated time that the prospect is to return. Speak to the prospect's secretary and explain your situation and the difficulty you are experiencing. If the secretary is also on voice mail, leave a message in the voice mail box as well. In rare instances, the secretary is authorized to make appointments for the decision maker. This approach is worth a try. You have nothing to lose and an appointment to gain.

Ask to speak to other individuals in the same department and develop a rapport with anyone who is even remotely in touch with the decision-maker that you are trying to reach. Try to find out if there is another individual, perhaps an assistant, with whom you can speak and perhaps arrange a meeting.

Try calling early in the morning, at coffee break time, during the lunch hour, afternoons or even late in the day.

When leaving those repetitious messages on the prospects' voice mail boxes, leave upbeat, friendly greetings that express optimism in making a connection.

In some cases, prospects might have access to two extensions. If, for example, the extension you have been given is #201 and you continuously receive voice mail at that extension, try dialing #202 or #200. It really does work sometimes. Even if another person answers, you have the opportunity to make yet another contact or track down he prospect.

Here is another last resort measure that can be employed. You can use it successfully on rare occasions when all reasonable efforts to reach a prospect have been exhausted. You contact the individual prospect's superior. Your intent is not to create problems for the individual involved, but simply to get the desired results for which you are highly paid.

One particularly innovative approach is to leave a message on the voice mail system that you are scheduling an unsolicited appointment with the prospect on a specific day at a specific time. Chances are very good that you will receive an immediate response. This approach can be effective if your company is well known in the industry.

Many of these last resort measures may be entirely new to you. They may frighten some and the may be scoffed at by the so-called "experts", but they work. Many salespeople dare not be different. They refuse to venture into the unknown and to walk on the edge. They buckle under pressure and refuse to stand up for their rights. You have to feel sorry for those individuals who will never experience the exquisite elation and satisfaction in turning adversity into victory. The decision is yours and yours alone.

How to Cope With Automated Answering Devices at the Reception Level

In today's complex business world, the live receptionist in many cases has gone the way of the dinosaur – and we call this "the age of communication"! This phrase is a misnomer in the true sense of the word. How do we cope with this blatant lack of public relations etiquette? It's not easy.

If you are calling long distance, it is not very prudent or cost effective to listen to a menu, listing personnel names and their extensions when you don't know to whom you should speak.

Save yourself a lot of aggravation and listen for the extension to the shipping department. Ask the person who answers to help connect you to the responsible individual and take note of the extension. Don't ever lose the extension number or you will have to start over.

Following are some further approaches to consider in reaching the decision maker in companies that employ automated answering.

If someone should eventually answer your initial enquiry and refuses to give you the name of the person who is responsible for a specific department, you might want to handle the problem in a number of ways.

1. Ask for the order department. When someone in the order department answers, offer an apology that you have the wrong extension and wanted to speak to the production manager. You then ask the individual to whom you are speaking to spell the managers last name.

2. Last but not least, if you run into an impregnable concrete wall that is seemingly impossible to penetrate and are unable to speak to anyone, here's what to do.

Leave your name, company name and number in the automated company voice mail box. Your message might imply that you might be interested in purchasing the prospect's product or service and that you wish to receive a call from the responsible person.

When a live voice does contact you, it is relatively easy to ask for an explanation of the company's product or service. At the conclusion of the brief overview, you simply state: that their service does not offer a fit for your company but that the products you sell could be of benefit to them. You then ask for the appropriate department and extension number.

You have finally secured the name of someone to whom you can speak and you will have acquired useful information to help you in your script preparation prior to making your phone presentation.

In order to survive you've got to be mentally tough. You must be cunning and able to exhibit a sense of creativity that will ensure that you will be remembered.

You must pursue your goals with an unquenchable thirst for success and find your own way.

XII.   SCRIPT PREPARATION FOR EMPLOYMENT OPPORTUNITIES

I truly believe that anyone – regardless of social status, job skills or educational background – can sell himself or herself on the phone to a prospective employer.

Let's first examine a job strategy plan for the unskilled high school drop out who has never held a full time job.

Scenario: A help wanted ad appears in the paper for unskilled or semi-skilled production workers. After the applicant secures the name of the production manager, I would suggest a script be developed as follows:

"Good morning .... My name is .... I'll just take a moment. Is that okay?

As a candidate for your production team, I bring a **wealth** of enthusiasm combined with **outstanding** motor skills, dexterity and adaptability to the XYZ Company.

One quick question:

If I could demonstrate a **strong** work ethic and the ability to learn quickly, could I introduce myself to you?

Wait for the Response

'Are mornings or afternoons best for you?

MAKE THE APPOINTMENT.

This script exhibits initiative, enthusiasm and drive. The person who delivered it has shown determination and a great deal of courage in making direct contact with the decision-maker. Do you think that a reasonably compassionate human being would agree to a brief meeting? I do.

Following are some samples of scripts that are customized for individuals who are seeking office positions.

Administrative Assistant

Good …………..! My name is …………..

I'll just take a moment of your time. Is that alright?

I'm a very competent person with a very **high** skill level in software and accounting programs.

One last comment:

If I could help your department to **substantially** increase efficiency levels, would you be interested?

Are mornings or afternoons best?

MAKE THE APPOINTMENT

Customer Service

Good …………..! My name is …………..

I'll just take a moment of your time. Is that okay?

I am an enthusiastic and friendly individual with **excellent** listening and communication skills. I have an extensive background in customer service.

One request:

If I could make a **real meaningful** contribution to your order department could we talk?

Close the appointment.

Data Entry

Following the standard introduction used in previous scripts state the following:

I have **outstanding keyboard** skills and offer **above average** computer knowledge.

Question.

If I could meet or **exceed** all deadlines could we talk?

Note: Close the appointment as in previous scripts.

Internet Representative

Following standard introduction state the following:

I am very **knowledgeable** with the Internet and its vast business potential.

One idea:

If I could **dramatically** expand your customer base, would you allow me to demonstrate my skills?

<u>Note</u>: Use the standard closing procedures.

Telephone Sales **(outbound)**

Following the standard introduction state the following:

I possess **above average** communication skills and am able to relate to **all** types of personalities at every level.

If I could meet or **exceed** all sales targets would you discuss this opportunity with me?

Close the appointment.

Accounting Representative

I am a reliable and flexible individual with a **solid** grasp of basic accounting procedures.

If I could offer **fast** and **accurate** document processing, could we discuss employment possibilities?

Courier

Following the standard introduction state the following:

I'm a self-starting individual with excellent communication skills and a strong sense of urgency in meeting customer deadlines.

If I could **guarantee** reliability AND flexibility would you meet with me for a few minutes?

Superintendent

I'm an individual who has a high degree of personal integrity with an extensive background in building maintenance procedures.

If I could make a **substantial** contribution to the maintenance management team could we get together?

Assistant Make-Up Artist

I have a **proven** flair for make-up fashion at **every** age level and have a proven background in theatrical productions.

If I could **enhance** your department with dedication and expertise, could we meet?

Housekeeping

I have a **fastidious** eye for detail in the area of personal property cleanliness.

If I could **guarantee** your complete satisfaction with every visit would you be willing to interview me?

High Tech Assembly (electronics)

I am an honors graduate in electronics and have a **natural** aptitude for electronic assembly and am very mechanically inclined.

If I could complement your production team with dedicated and **productive** output, could we get together for a few minutes?

Warning:
Please remember one thing! Always, just get a commitment for a meeting. Meetings are the proper venue for the discussion of details.
Brevity, regardless of your knowledge, your intellect or your expertise, is the key to success when developing employment prospects via the telephone.

Script Tips

A number of the sample scripts shown can be rewritten by interchanging your opening statement with the **hook** or closing statement.

For example, the last script on *High Tech Assembly* could be written as follows:

I am a dedicated and productive electronics graduate who could compliment your team with additional productivity output.

One comment:

If I could exhibit a natural ability for electronics assembly, along with a mechanical aptitude, could we meet?

By constantly interchanging your opening and closing statements, you will keep the script fresh and will be assured of maximum impact. Dozens of combinations are possible using this method.

If you are an individual seeking employment in other fields of endeavour, the aforementioned sample scripts can be rewritten to reflect your own individual skills to secure that all important first interview.

If, for example, you are seeking employment in the computer education field, consider the following script:

Good ....! Mr./Mrs. .... My name is ....

I'll be brief. Is that okay/

In response to your ad for a software trainer, I have **extensive** experience at the corporate level.

I have a **proven** ability to maximize individual performance levels through dedicated support and direction.

If I could make a **substantial** contribution to your team of software training specialist, could we get together for 15 minutes?

Financial Service

Good ....! Mr./Mrs. .... My name is .... You don't know me, so I'll be brief! Is that okay.

I have **impeccable** credentials as a senior level banker in international banking circles. My background includes numerous successful loan negotiations with high-ranking company executives at both the national and international level.

If I could make a **significant** contribution to bottom-line results, could we get together for a few minutes?

Accounting

Good ....! Mr./Mrs. .... My name is ....

I'll be brief! Is that okay?

As a certified general accountant, I offer **outstanding** expertise in management, finance and guidance in government assistance and training programs.

If I could **dramatically** increase your customer base in the independent business sector, could we meet for a few minutes?

Personnel Placement Agency

Good ....! Mr./Mrs. .... My name is ....

I'll just take a moment. Is that alright?

My educational background and practical experience in the areas of pay equity, salary surveys and management placements is **well documented** throughout the industrial business sector.

If I could **prove** my worth to your company in these three vital areas, would you allow me 15 minutes of your time?

Newspaper

Good ....! Mr./Mrs. .... My name is ....

You don't know me, so I'll be brief! Is that okay?

I have an **extensive** knowledge of the seniors market as a representative of a competitive newspaper. I can offer valuable expertise in the areas of prospect lead generation, and verifiable closing skills.

If I could meet or **exceed** any and all sales objectives, could we get together for 15 minutes?

The employment scripts that you have just read are a natural extension of the previous sample scripts. The skills that you have learned are transferable to any industry, for any purpose. The methodology employed in these scripts can even be used for e-mail communication and job interviews.

It is very important to insert the prospective employer's name throughout the script. This simple inclusion will guarantee that your prospect is listening to the presentation.

All of the scripts that you have read, although designed for entirely different jobs have several things in common. Pause, for a moment if you will, and list them on a note pad.

If you mentioned brevity score one correct answer. If you mentioned the fact that all scripts strictly highlighted persona attributes you are on your way to becoming employed. The other common traits that these scripts possess include a sense of urgency, a sincere promise of results, and an overwhelming desire to be of service.

Should a prospective employer request a resume via e-mail before granting an interview, ask the responsible individual to set a firm date and time for a meeting to discuss the resume with you. If your request is denied, follow up within five days in order to secure an appointment.

*****

The sole objective of this training guide has been to impart innovative ideas that get positive results in communicating with other individuals. Review the contents of "The Call Wizard" on a regular basis and your vision of success will become reality.